Y^BH*

Yes, But How?

BOX 3566 • GRAND RAPIDS. MI 49501

**PUBLISHING BOOKS THAT FEED
THE SOUL WITH THE WORD OF GOD.**

Yes, But How?

Getting Serious About Your Faith

Vernon C. Grounds

Yes, But How?
Getting Serious About Your Faith
Copyright © 1991 by Vernon C. Grounds

Library of Congress Cataloging-in-Publication Data

Grounds, Vernon C.
  Yes, but how? : getting serious about your faith /
Vernon C. Grounds
    p.   cm.
    ISBN 0-929239-50-4
    1. Christian life—1960. I. Title.
BV4501.G793 1991
248.4—dc20   91-21255
                                                    CIP

Discovery House Publishers is affiliated with
Radio Bible Class, Grand Rapids, Michigan

Printed in the United States of America

91 92 93 94 95 / CHG / 10 9 8 7 6 5 4 3 2 1

Contents

Foreword

I WAS BROWSING in a bookstore when I stumbled on a car repair manual with an intriguing subtitle: *A Book for Mechanics Who Don't Know the First Thing about Cars.* That was my kind of book! If repairing our automobile depended on my mechanical skill, our family would never leave home. I knew the book was written for me when a chapter on changing a tire began, "First, insert the key in the trunk and open it." Now that's getting down to basics.

For a long time we have needed a manual like that on the Christian life. Many volumes on the subject are designed for theologians who, like master mechanics, don't really need them. Some books are aimed at saintly types who have already arrived or who live in another century—or worse, in another world. Others make the Christian life sound as rigid and complicated as instructions for assembling a computer.

In this book, Dr. Vernon Grounds has written for Christians who feel they don't know the first thing about living a productive Christian life and would like to find out. He starts at the level of "insert the key in the trunk and open it" and goes on from there. I expect to put this book into the hands of fledgling Christians who want to make a good start in their relationship with Christ, but I also plan to recommend it to weathered veterans of the faith as well. As Vince Lombardi, the great coach of the Green Bay Packers, used to say, "Whenever you get away from the fundamentals, you've gone a long way toward defeat." Fundamentals. That's what this book is about—the fundamentals for the life all of us were created to live.

Haddon W. Robinson
Distinguished Professor, Harold J. Ockenga
Chair of Preaching, Gordon-Conwell Seminary

Preface

A BOOK LOVER once lent one of his prized volumes to a friend. The friend, upon returning it, confessed his puzzlement. As he had turned its pages, he had noticed in the margins the cryptic initials YBH, followed by a question mark. *YBH?* So he asked his friend, "What is the meaning of that symbol you have jotted down in the margins of so many pages, YBH?"

With a smile the book lover explained, "Oh, that means, 'Yes, but how?' I will be reading along, and I will agree with what the author writes, only I wonder about making his ideas work in life. 'Yes. But how?' "

It's a good question, isn't it? *"Yes. But how?"* How do you change print into flesh-and-blood reality? How do you take a truth and translate it into action? YBH? So with ourselves. We want to be disciples of Jesus. We want to be productive Christians. We want to bear much fruit to the glory of God. We want all those gracious characteristics exhibited by our Lord to be reproduced in our own behavior.

This book is intended to address ten essential principles of productivity and growth for those who take their Christian faith seriously. Then I aim to answer that all-important question of application, "Yes, but how?" If to any degree this voluume stimulates Christlike character and action, I will be thankful indeed.

Vernon Grounds

PRINCIPLE ONE

A Supernatural Change of Nature

PICK UP A BIBLE that someone has used for years—one that has been lovingly carried, thumbed, and studied. You may discover that the margin is darkest at John's gospel, chapters 14 through 16.

No wonder! This is the Upper Room Discourse, the remarkable conversation Jesus had with His disciples on the night of His betrayal. In the fifteenth chapter, verse 8, He said, "This is to my Father's glory, that you bear much fruit, showing yourselves to be my disciples." That is a statement we need to reflect upon—repeatedly and thoughtfully—through the moments and days of our lives.

As we ponder this verse, it will be helpful to ask ourselves a question. It's a familiar question to many—one that comes from the Westminster Shorter Catechism: *"What is the chief end of man?"* Those words were drafted in seventeenth-century England by a notable company of theologians and pastors. They met at Westminster to clarify what they as Protestants believed about the Christian faith. One of the historic documents they composed was the Shorter Catechism, the one that begins with that disturbing, all-important question. What *is* the chief end of man? The men who met at Westminster answered the question in language that is very simple—yet profound in its simplicity: *"Man's chief end is to glorify God, and to enjoy him for ever."* That's worth memorizing. That's worth contemplating daily. The chief purpose for which we are living is what? To glorify God and enjoy Him forever.

But immediately, still pondering John 15:8, we confront a second question. How is it possible for us sinful, finite creatures to glorify God? How can we—with all our limitations—add anything at all to the majesty and the blessedness of the everlasting Creator? It seems so impossible. Almost incredible. Yet Jesus assures us that we can glorify God—by "bearing much fruit." It is through such spiritual productivity, He says, that we become His disciples. Maybe, then, we should make a distinction. Of course faith—and faith plus nothing else—secures our forgiveness and brings us into an eternally right relationship with God. But maybe there are Christians who, though born again by faith, never grow beyond the stage of inactive belief. They fail to progress spiritually into the category of discipleship. For only productive Christians are entitled to be called disciples.

What is the supreme purpose of human life? A Christlike discipleship that glorifies God. And how do we become Christlike disciples? By bearing fruit. No, by bearing *much* fruit, becoming maximally productive for the praise of our heavenly Father.

But what is *fruit*? The word calls to mind apple orchards in September or a well-stocked produce aisle at the supermarket. Branches and trees, bushes and vines. What does all that have to do with the experience of Christian living? The apostle Paul talks about this special kind of fruit in Galatians 5:22–23. The list he comes up with sounds even more attractive and desirable than Washington apples or Michigan cherries. The fruit of the Spirit, he writes, is "love, joy, peace, patience, kindness, goodness, faithfulness, gentleness and self-control." The apostle here gives us a kind of catalog, an inventory of Christlike characteristics. And as we develop these personality traits and exhibit these characteristics by the enablement of the Holy Spirit, we glorify God.

This brings us to our fourth question. How is it possible for us to produce this Christlike fruit in our lives? As we begin to grapple with that question, let's look back at an all-important first-century interview.

One night Nicodemus, a leading Jew and a Pharisee, came to see Jesus.

15

"Rabbi," he began, "we realize that you are a teacher who has come from God. For no one could show the signs that you show unless God were with him."

"Believe me," returned Jesus, "when I assure you that a man cannot see the kingdom of God without being born again."

"And how can a man who has grown old possibly be born?" replied Nicodemus. "Surely he cannot go into his mother's womb a second time to be born?"

"I do assure you," said Jesus, "that unless a man is born from water and from spirit he cannot enter the kingdom of God. Flesh gives birth to flesh and spirit gives birth to spirit: you must not be surprised that I told you that all of you must be born again. The wind blows where it likes, you can hear the sound of it but you have no idea where it comes from or where it goes. Nor can you tell how a man is born by the wind of the Spirit."

"How on earth can things like this happen?" replied Nicodemus.

"So you are the teacher of Israel," said Jesus, "and you do not understand such things? I assure you that we are talking about what we know and we are witnessing to what we have observed, yet you will not accept our evidence. Yet if I have spoken to you about things that happen on this earth and you will not believe me, what chance is there that you will believe me if I tell you about what happens in Heaven? No one has ever been up to Heaven except

16

*the Son of Man who came down from Heaven. The
Son of Man must be lifted above the heads of
men—as Moses lifted up that serpent in the
desert—so that any man who believes in him may
have eternal life. For God loved the world so much
that he gave his only Son, so that everyone who
believes in him should not be lost, but should have
eternal life"* (John 3:1–16 PHILLIPS).

Nicodemus was perplexed. Judaism he knew. But
this? What could the Teacher mean by "a new birth"?
How could a grown man return to his mother's womb
and start all over again?

In His answer to this searching Pharisee, Jesus
explained that the new birth takes place through the
power of the Spirit when we believe in Himself as Savior,
uplifted on the cross as a sacrifice for our sins. Verse 7 is
pivotal. Jesus declared to His perplexed visitor, "Do not
marvel that I said to you [singular], 'You [plural] must
be born anew.' " The shift from singular to plural is
crucial. Our Lord's imperative is all-inclusive: *everyone,*
with no exceptions, must be born again. But that
imperative plunged Nicodemus into deeper perplexity.
What was the logic of this all-inclusive command?

According to the Bible, we are born into the world
with a fallen nature that we inherit from our parents
who inherited it from their parents who inherited it
from their parents . . . . Well, push the line of human
ancestry back, back, back to Adam and Eve, who
committed the first sin and who transmitted a fallen

17

nature to their children. As descendents of that fallen couple, we are born corrupt, depraved. In fact, we are born in a state of *total depravity*. This does not mean we are evil through and through like an apple that is thoroughly rotten. It means, rather, that our whole being has been infected and affected by inherited sin. Total depravity might better be called "total inability." Born with a fallen nature, we cannot do, neither can we be, what we ought to do and be until we are born again. The miracle of that new birth changes us within. It changes both our relationship to God and our eternal destiny. By the power of the Holy Spirit we are enabled to be what God wants us to be and to do what God wants us to do.

Why, then, must everyone be born again? Only by that supernatural transformation can total inability be replaced by the capacity to be and to do what God wants. Only by this life-changing miracle are we able to become productive for His praise.

The teaching of Jesus in Matthew clears away any lingering perplexity.

> *By their fruit you will recognize them. Do people pick grapes from thornbushes, or figs from thistles? Likewise every good tree bears good fruit, but a bad tree bears bad fruit. A good tree cannot bear bad fruit, and a bad tree cannot bear good fruit. Every tree that does not bear good fruit is cut down and thrown into the fire. Thus, by their fruit you will recognize them* (7:16–20).

Jesus is not talking here about literal trees—the bark and branch variety. He is talking, instead, about people—the whole human race, including you and me. So if we are going to become good trees, bearing fruit for the praise of God, a miracle must occur. There must be a supernatural change within, a supernatural change that takes place when, believing in the Savior uplifted on the cross, we are born again.

Let us examine more closely the fallen condition of "total depravity" that makes us barren trees, totally unable to bear spiritual fruit. In our natural fallen state, we can't even *see* spiritual realities. Jesus said as much to His night visitor in John 3:3: "Unless one is born again, he cannot see the kingdom of God" (NKJV). This is not a reference to the future, warning that, unless a person is born again, he will never get a glimpse of glory. No, it refers to a *present* affliction. Until we undergo this miraculous transformation, all of us are spiritually blind: We cannot see supernatural realities.

Project yourself into this situation: You are carefully and lovingly explaining to a friend the grace of God in Jesus Christ. A very intelligent person, that friend shakes his head negatively and responds, "I just don't see it." What is your friend really doing? He is admitting his inability to perceive supernatural realities. And they are realities. A rose is a reality, yet its beauty is invisible to a blind person. In the same way, until we are born again, you and I are spiritually blind.

But our handicaps don't end there. We are also spiritually deaf. Until we are born again we cannot *hear*

19

the Word of God. That may strike us as strange, but in John's gospel Jesus asks, "Why do you not understand my words?" And immediately He answers His own question, "It is because you cannot hear what I am really saying" (John 8:43 PHILLIPS). Now clearly He addressed an audience with functioning physical ears. They had auditory equipment as good as yours and mine. But because they were dead in trespasses and sins, those listeners lacked the ability to hear God's truth. And that is a universal affliction, the plight of everyone who has not yet been born again. A man may sit in church listening attentively, but he is unable to grasp the spiritual meaning of what he heard. Neither can we until we are born again. However acute our hearing may be, God's truth does not penetrate. We are spiritually deaf.

Paul sums up our total inability in a letter to the Corinthian believers: "The man without the Spirit does not accept the things that come from the Spirit of God, for they are foolishness to him, and he cannot understand them, because they are spiritually discerned" (1 Corinthians 2:14). The "man without the Spirit" is anyone and everyone, male or female, young or old, who has never experienced the second birth. They are spiritual vegetables. They may be blessed with high IQ's. They may have impressive educational backgrounds, with a string of degrees behind their names. But until each one is born again, he cannot receive the things of the Spirit of God. In fact, Paul affirms, those things are foolishness to him. He cannot know them because they are understandable only with the Spirit's help.

Why, therefore, must everyone be born again? All of us are affected with total inability. We cannot see God's reality. We cannot hear God's truth. We cannot understand God's Word. It is through the new birth that our inability is taken away and we are enabled to do what God wants us to do and to be what God wants us to be. That miracle transforms our natures, changing us into good trees capable of bearing Christlike fruit—fruit that brings glory to God.

Furthermore, according to the New Testament, the once-born individual cannot do anything that is spiritually good. He may do social good and do it tirelessly. But it is impossible for a person to do anything spiritually good until he receives new life from Christ.

As Paul cries out: "I know that nothing good lives in me, that is, in my sinful nature. For I have the desire to do what is good, but I cannot carry it out. For I do not the good I want to do; no, the evil I do not want to do—this I keep on doing. Now if I do what I do not want to do, it is no longer I who do it, but it is sin living in me that does it" (Romans 7:18–20).

Jeremiah echoes Paul's cry: "Can the Ethiopian change his skin or the leopard its spots? Neither can you do good who are accustomed to doing evil" (13:23).

It is impossible for the once-born person to do anything spiritually good. He is incapable of behavior motivated by love, obedience, and faith, a life that brings praise to God and wins God's commendation.

Now there is yet one more thing to learn about our spiritual barrenness: "Those controlled by the sinful

21

nature cannot please God" (Romans 8:8). To be controlled by the sinful nature is to be once-born, crippled by a fallen nature, in rebellion against God, stubbornly refusing to do the one thing God demands— admit that we are sinners, hopelessly lost unless we believe the gospel. To be controlled by the sinful nature is to live as an unbeliever and to ignore the disturbing truth of God's Word: "Without faith it is impossible to please God" (Hebrews 11:6).

A further consequence of our plight without Christ is the inability to experience real happiness. This isn't to say that non-Christians can't enjoy themselves immensely. All of us are acquainted with unbelieving friends who seem to be getting as great a kick out of life as we are. But the truth stands: We cannot experience real happiness, authentic inner joy, until we are born again. "The kingdom of God," says Paul, "is not a matter of eating and drinking but of righteousness, peace and joy in the Holy Spirit" (Romans 14:17). Yet until we are born again, we cannot experience these things. We can know a measure of happiness, to be sure, but in the words of an old hymn,

> *Solid joys and lasting pleasures*
> *Only Zion's children know.*

And Zion's children are those people who, by faith in Jesus Christ and by the power of the Holy Spirit, have been born again and have entered into the kingdom of God.

Finally, what is the tragic outcome of our total inability to see God's reality, hear God's Word, understand supernatural truth, do spiritual good, please God, and experience authentic happiness? Listen to the warning of Jesus: "I am going away, and you will look for me, and you will die in your sin. Where I go, you cannot come" (John 8:21). And where was Jesus going? He was going to heaven, where all is perfect peace and unblemished joy. So the final tragedy of our total inability is the inability to go where Jesus is. That tragedy, however, can be averted. By the miracle of regeneration —the new birth—we too can enter into the presence of God, rejoicing with Jesus forever and ever.

Why, then, did the Savior tell Nicodemus, "You must be born again?" Until we are born again, we are bad trees, incapable of bearing fruit that will please God.

All the questions we have been considering confront us with an inescapable question, a question each one of us must ask and answer in the secret place of our inner selves. Have I been born again? Have I as a lost sinner knelt at the cross? Have I acknowledged that I have no hope apart from the death of Jesus for my sins?

John Wesley preached and preached on the text, "You must be born again." A woman heard him preach about it three times. After the third sermon, she bustled up to the fervent evangelist and, with some impatience, demanded, "Mr. Wesley, why must you always preach on that text, 'You must be born again'?"

"Because madam," he replied, "you must be born again."

Wesley was right. It is this very miracle that transforms us into good trees with the potential to bear fruit for God's glory.

PRINCIPLE TWO

A Dynamic Adjustment to the Holy Spirit

THOUGH THEY WERE sincere believers, the early Christians from Ephesus were relatively uninstructed. They believed in God the Father, and of course they believed in Jesus as Savior. But, according to the book of Acts, they were ignorant of one vital truth.

> *While Apollos was at Corinth, Paul took the road through the interior and arrived at Ephesus. There he found some disciples and asked them, "Did you receive the Holy Spirit when you believed?"*

> *They answered, "No, we have not even heard that*
> *there is a Holy Spirit"* (19:1–2).

Unfortunately, even today some Christians are like that. They believe in God, the eternal Creator. They believe He never started to exist because He had existed forever and forever in eternity past. They believe, too, that God will exist forever and forever in eternity future. They believe that God is all-powerful, all-wise, all-loving, all-good. But Jews believe that. Muslims believe that. Unitarians believe that.

What is distinctive, then, about our faith in God? We are trinitarians. We believe that God is one, and yet in the infinite riches of His being God is three persons existing in unity. We believe in God the Father. We believe in God the Son. We believe in God the Holy Spirit. We confess our faith every time we sing:

> *Holy, Holy, Holy, Lord God Almighty!*
> *Early in the morning our songs shall rise to Thee;*
> *Holy, Holy, Holy! Merciful and Mighty!*
> *God in Three Persons, blessed Trinity!*

A Sunday school teacher may courageously attempt the impossible. Deciding to explain the mystery of the Triune Godhead to her perceptive pupils, she may resort to a simple explanation that simply doesn't explain:

> *Three in One and One in Three,*
> *And the One in the middle died for me.*

26

That is true, of course. But explain the Trinity? We can't even begin. We can only accept it—a mystery, disclosed in Scripture. It should be no surprise that the triune Being of God baffles our finite minds. We should be surprised, rather, if we *could* understand the nature of our Creator. He would be a two-bit deity, not the fathomless Source of all reality.

Suppose an earthworm were able to think. It certainly would be puzzled by human beings. That reflective creature might attend a convocation of philosophical earthworms and argue, "There cannot be any such composite being as a man. A mind-body entity is utterly illogical. How can mind, something immaterial, co-exist with body, which is something material? Therefore, human beings do not exist—or at least they are not composite creatures." Beyond all philosophical convocations and arguments, however, our God exists. And He exists eternally as three co-equal persons, Father, Son, and Holy Spirit. That is a basic fact, and while we do not fathom it, we hold to it unwaveringly.

Two great truths about one of those divine Persons, the Holy Spirit, have the power to unleash in us awesome potential for productive living.

The Holy Spirit indwells every believer

Jesus looked at the men who reclined with Him around the supper table. Time was slipping away. The words He spoke at that last meal would have to sustain these men for the torturous hours—and the long years of ministry—ahead. He wanted to comfort them in their anxiety and grief. He wanted them to understand, and He wanted you and me to understand as well.

> *I shall ask the Father to give you Someone else to stand by you, to be with you always. I mean the Spirit of truth, whom the world cannot accept, for it can neither see nor recognize that Spirit. But you recognize him, for he is with you now and is in your hearts. I am not going to leave you alone in the world—I am coming to you. In a very little while, the world will see me no more but you will see me, because I am really alive and you will be alive too. When that day comes, you will realize that I am in my Father, that you are in me, and I am in you.*
>
> *Every man who knows my commandments and obeys them is the man who really loves me, and every man who really loves me will himself be loved by my Father, and I too will love him and make myself known to him* (John 14:16–21 PHILLIPS).

The meaning of this stunning promise is clear. The Holy Spirit, another Comforter, was coming to live in every disciple, making real the presence of Jesus and the presence of the Father—not for a limited time but forever.

Paul also teaches this incredible, encouraging truth. He writes: "Do you not know that your body is a temple of the Holy Spirit within you, who is in you, whom you have received from God?" (1 Corinthians 6:19). So every believer, though an ordinary disciple, is by no means an ordinary person. He is a temple of the Holy Spirit. What a mind-staggering thought! Where does God live by His Holy Spirit? Where do you find the presence of Jesus through the Holy Spirit? Visit London and walk through the magnificent St. Paul's Cathedral. Or visit Paris and gaze in amazement at the Cathedral of Notre Dame. Or when in Los Angeles let the Crystal Cathedral dazzle you. These structures are impressive, but none of them is the temple of God.

Lift up your head. Straighten your shoulders. Walk with pride and gratitude. You, believer, have the Spirit living within. You are the very temple of the living God!

As an old hymn reminds us:

> *Joys are flowing like a river,*
> *Since the Comforter has come;*
> *He abides with us forever,*
> *Makes the trusting heart His home.*

Every believer is the Spirit's home. He lives within, not as a temporary Guest but as a permanent Resident.

But there is a second great truth to consider—one that is as gripping and potentially life-changing as the first.

Every believer can be filled by the Holy Spirit

Paul holds out before us this enticing possibility: "Do not get drunk on wine, which leads to debauchery.

Instead be filled with the Spirit" (Ephesians 5:18). Actually he is exhorting, "*Keep on being filled* with the Spirit." The verb is progressive, implying that the "filling" is continuous.

But how can you and I be filled with the Spirit? How can you and I be so yielded to the Spirit that He possesses us, empowers us, controls us, and guides us? We do so by a two-step process. Step one is *cleansing*. Step two is *claiming*.

Once in a while as guest-preacher I find myself getting thirsty. I look around for a glass of water on a shelf in the pulpit, hidden from the congregation's sight. Ah, I do discover a glass! But—the water has been sitting there two weeks perhaps. It is stagnant, unfit for drinking. Before I use a glass like that it must be emptied and cleaned, even scoured. Then it can be filled and become a means of refreshment. In the same way, before the Spirit's filling can take place in our lives, there must be an emptying and cleansing. The apostle John speaks to this very point: "If we refuse to admit that we are sinners, then we live in a world of illusion and truth becomes a stranger to us. But if we freely admit that we have sinned, we find him reliable and just—he forgives our sins and makes us thoroughly clean from all that is evil" (1 John 1:8–9 PHILLIPS).

The second step in the process is claiming. Our Lord said:

> *Ask and it will be given to you; seek and you will find; knock and the door will be opened to you. For*

everyone who asks receives; he who seeks finds; and to him who knocks, the door will be opened. Which of you fathers, if your son asks for a fish, will give him a snake instead? Or if he asks for an egg, will give him a scorpion? If you then, though you are evil, know how to give good gifts to your children, how much more will your Father in heaven give the Holy Spirit to those who ask him! (Luke 11:9–13).

We need not ask for the Spirit's indwelling, but we do need to ask for His filling. We need to ask with intensity. We need to ask with expectancy. We need to ask with a deep, overwhelming sense of our need.

But why do we even ask? What is the purpose of the Spirit's filling? Just this: We cannot live productive lives—we cannot bear fruit—without the enablement of God's Spirit. The whole cluster of Christlike characteristics that God yearns to have us produce in our lives is the fruit of the Spirit. This helps us understand Paul's bold and daring parallel command: "Do not be intoxicated; keep on being filled." Most of us have not been alcoholics. We have not been bothered by a problem that for some of our friends has been agonizing. But what do we observe in a person with this problem? Sober, this person may be cowardly. Sober, he may be almost tongue-tied. Sober, he may be very selfish. But get him drunk, and the coward becomes courageous; the tongue-tied person becomes talkative; the penny-pincher becomes thoughtlessly generous. Intoxication produces an about-face personality change, a release from inhibitions.

The book of Acts paints this startling picture of a Spirit-filled church:

> *After they prayed, the place where they were meeting was shaken. And they were all filled with the Holy Spirit and spoke the word of God boldly.*
>
> *All the believers were one in heart and mind. No one claimed that any of his possessions was his own, but they shared everything they had* (4:31–32).

These ordinary people, filled with the Spirit, became extraordinary. Once they had been cowards, afraid of persecution, hiding behind locked doors. But filled with the Spirit, they were brave enough to face martyrdom. Once they had been hesitant about bearing witness to Jesus. But Spirit-filled, they went out into the streets and began to proclaim the good news with great effectiveness. Spirit-filled, they forgot about their own future needs and pooled their resources to help meet the immediate needs of others. What a challenging model for churches today! The same Holy Spirit who charged first-century saints with joy and boldness is equally available to you and me in these declining days of the twentieth century. Spirit-filled, we can work together in unity and power, liberated from selfish concerns and supernaturally energized to witness and serve.

One day a parishioner entered the study of F. B. Meyer, the well-known English preacher, to sign an important document. Lying on the pastor's desk was a fountain pen, an instrument regarded at that time as a remarkable invention. The parishioner picked it up to write his signature, but Dr. Meyer restrained him. "Don't try using that," he said with a smile. "I call it my castaway. It refuses to be filled." Meyer's casual comment was a sermon in itself. He illustrated 1 Corinthians 9:27, where Paul warns against the danger of becoming a spiritual castaway, and he underscored Ephesians 5:18, where Paul exhorts believers to "keep on being filled with the Spirit." If we refuse to do that—or neglect to do that—we are not in danger of being cast away eternally, but we are in danger of being set aside by God as an instrument He cannot use.

Set aside. Shelved. Benched. What a tragic waste of potential! What a denial of all that God longs for us to do and be for the name of His Son. Let us cry out to our Father to so fill us with His Spirit that our lives brim over, spilling His life and joy like refreshing rain on a tired and cynical planet. And let us live in such a way that He will be pleased to grant our hearts' desires.

PRINCIPLE THREE

A Daily Death to the Self-Life

DO YOU SUPPOSE God is in the business of making Christians feel cheap and worthless? Does He make it His job to put Christians down until they have no self-confidence, no self-esteem, no self-respect? What a warped idea! God certainly is *not* in the business of reducing Christians to zero.

The case is different, of course, with people who have not yet invited Jesus Christ into their lives. God *is* in the business of convicting such people that they are inadequate, helplessly incapable of doing what He wants them to do and being what He wants them to be. Yes, God is in the business of so awakening unconverted human beings to the depths of their need that they agree with Isaiah, "All of our righteous acts are like filthy rags." He is in the business of humbling self-sufficient sinners so they admit that their moral best is fit for nothing except the cosmic garbage dump, so that they voluntarily say to Jesus:

> *Nothing in my hands I bring;*
> *Simply to thy Cross I cling.*

But after a person has accepted Christ and been born anew, what then? Does God engage in a relentless process of deflating Christians like some prankster puncturing a child's balloon? Is He pleased when a sincere believer has a poor self-image? Unfortunately, that is the impression many believers pick up in their reading of the New Testament. Being spiritual, they conclude, means denying yourself, hating yourself, crucifying yourself—psychic suicide. Any positive feelings about ourselves must be killed off. Any good opinions about who we are and what we can do must be exterminated—like bugs in a garden. This widespread impression accounts for the confusion and conflict some of us needlessly experience. It explains why we are not sure what to believe about ourselves or how we ought to act.

Conflict and confusion? Indeed. In Matthew 19:19 we hear God commanding us to love our neighbors as we love ourselves. We assume, therefore, that self-love is not wrong. And then we read in John 10:10 that Jesus came that we might enjoy abundant life. So we assume that God wants us to be genuinely happy and fulfilled. We read further, in 1 Corinthians 15:10, Paul's forthright claim that he has worked harder than all the other apostles: he has done more for the Lord than Peter or James or anyone else. This leads us to assume that it is right for a Christian to engage in honest self-praise.

But that is only one side of the coin. There is another side found in the New Testament. Luke 14:26 brings us up short! This text seems to rule out anything even resembling self-love. Laying down the conditions of discipleship, Jesus declared, "If any one comes to me and does not hate his own father and mother, his wife and children, his brothers and sisters—yes, even his own life—he cannot be my disciple." This text confuses us. Self-hate or self-love? Which does God approve? What is He really asking of us?

Reading on, we note in John 12:24–25 that Jesus said, "Unless a kernel of wheat falls to the ground and dies, it remains only a single seed. But if it dies, it produces many seeds. The man who loves his life will lose it, while the man who hates his life in this world will keep it for eternal life." Again, we are confused. Self-love or self-hate? Which does God want? What does He require? How does dying enable us to live—and to live productively? We are up against a problem that perplexes us and cries out for a solution.

The solution, however, is quite simple. God is not in

the business of breaking Christians down, reducing them to zeros. God is in the business of building Christians up, maximizing their talents, and fulfilling their potential. He is not out to diminish selfhood. By no means! Selfhood is what you and I are as human beings created in God's image. Not only that, if we are Christians we have been redeemed by the precious blood of our Lord, we are indwelt by the Holy Spirit, and we are guaranteed ultimate conformity to Jesus. God, then, is in the business of making us the happiest, the best, the most productive persons we can be. But to maximize our selfhood, God has to help us get rid of our self-centeredness, our self-concern, our sinful selfishness. God has to help us relinquish our self-centered hopes, dreams, ambitions, wants, and desires.

To put it succinctly, God has to help us to develop the Gethsemane mind-set, that attitude demonstrated by Jesus Christ on the night of His betrayal. In Matthew 26 we become spectators of a battle that our Lord fought in the darkness of the garden as His disciples slept—a violent, wrenching conflict with forces, issues, and emotions beyond our comprehension. Although fully God, Jesus was a real Man. His human nature was no masquerade. It was the same as yours and mine, except that Jesus was sinless. Yet being genuinely human, our Lord longed to sidestep death. Motivated by our common instinct of self-preservation, He wanted to run away from shame, disgrace, humiliation, intolerable pain of body, and agony of soul. In His human nature He desperately yearned to escape the cross. And yet in the face of these overpowering emotions, standing on the very edge of unutterable suffering and horror, He spoke those unforgettable words of self-abandonment: "My Father, if it is possible let this cup pass from me—yet it must not be what I want, but what you want" (Matthew 26:39 PHILLIPS).

Jesus said *no* to His own will and *yes* to His Father's will. He did this in faith, believing that obedient suffering would bring fullness of joy and blessing in the victory of the resurrection. In the words of Hebrews 12:2, He, the Author and Perfecter of our faith, endured the cross, thinking nothing of its shame because of His confidence that beyond sorrow lay joy, beyond death was endless life, beyond the Roman gibbet gleamed the glory of God's throne.

What, then, is the Gethsemane mind-set? It is the attitude of trustful self-surrender demonstrated by Jesus as He prayed, "Not my will, Father, but your will be done." It is the renunciation of our own very human feelings, desires, hopes, dreams, and ambitions that the purposes of God may be accomplished. We develop this mind-set as we follow the example of Jesus. We set our minds on doing the will of God, obeying Him even though obedience involves self-denial, the surrender of anything that would interfere with the fulfillment of the divine purpose. We do this in the confidence that, as we follow our Lord's example, we are going to experience, beyond loss and loneliness and pain, the joy and blessing and glory that mean unimaginable self-fulfillment.

Sometimes a chapter out of someone's life story

39

opens a floodgate of light and understanding. Take a moment to consider pivotal episodes from the lives of three very fruitful Christians.

Mildred Cable

Mildred Cable grew up in Great Britain, a deeply dedicated, single-minded disciple, headed for a ministry to China. But she met a fellow-disciple and fell in love with him. He more than returned her love and naturally wanted to marry her. Mildred, though, was convinced God was leading her to China. The man she loved, however, was equally convinced God wanted him to remain in England to serve there as a pastor. They prayed, talked, and wept together, but neither could sense the freedom to abandon what seemed to be the definite will of God. One night they kissed each other good-bye and with heartbreak ended their relationship. Mildred's biographer concludes that chapter in her life with one terse sentence: "That night she died." Oh, she went on living long years afterward, but that night she died to her own desires, her own hopes, her own humanly legitimate dreams. She died to her own will to carry out the will of God. She went to China where God gave her the joy and blessing of an extraordinarily fruitful ministry.

George Muller

Muller's biographer, A. T. Pierson, marvels at how this "one poor man" in Bristol, England, "dependent on the help of God only in answer to prayer," had in his lifetime cared for over 10,000 orphans, building five spacious homes to house them. He established day-schools and Sunday schools all over the world in which perhaps 150,000 children had been taught; he put into circulation 2 million Bibles and Scripture portions; he published more than 3 million books and tracts; and in addition he liberally supported missionaries in many countries. So in his sixty years of remarkable ministry he had been entrusted by God with the stewardship of gifts that Pierson, writing in 1899, estimated must have amounted to $7.5 million. Imagine how much that would be today!

What was the secret of Muller's phenomenally fruitful service for God and the human family Christ died to redeem? Asked that very question by a grateful admirer, he replied, bending lower and lower until almost touching the floor, "There was a day when I died, *utterly died,* died to George Muller, his opinions, preferences, tastes, and will—died to the world, its approval or censure; died to the approval or blame even of my brethren and friends—and since then I have studied only to show myself approved to God."

Frank Laubach

Through the reading techniques he developed, Frank Laubach made it possible for millions of illiterates to hear God speaking to them in their own language. But in the early years of his ministry, he was a missionary in the Philippines—an unhappy, defeated Christian. He hated the very people to whom he was witnessing. They were dirty, betel-nut chewers. Unresponsive. Offensive to his eyes and nose.

Late one afternoon in a mood of despondency and despair, Laubach climbed a high hill above the city of Manila. Sitting there alone, he thought of all the futile years he had spent in the Philippines, miserable and unproductive years. He thought of the obnoxious people to whom the Lord had sent him, people he despised in his heart. Overcome with self-pity, he crouched on that lonely hill and wept—his body shaking with sobs. As he sat there crying he began to pray like Elijah, "Lord, let me die. Let me die." But slowly the Spirit of God convicted him of his conceit and sinful selfishness. At last, blessedly broken, he fell down on his knees and surrendered himself to Jesus.

As he often said afterward, "That night Frank Laubach died." And die he did. He died to his old attitudes, his old feelings, his old sinful self-pity and hateful pride. And that night he became a different man. He became a loving and much-loved missionary, a productive servant of Jesus Christ with a global ministry, honored and esteemed by mighty and lowly alike. Frank Laubach, like Mildred Cable and George Muller, gives life and breath to a cornerstone New Testament principle: *Death to the self-life is a condition of spiritual productivity.*

Are you and I honestly willing to trust God? Do we believe He never asks any child of His to make a senseless sacrifice? Do we believe that? Do we believe that in the long run obedience to the Father's will is going to bring deep and joyous fulfillment?

42

No matter what you've heard or read, however, self-surrender is not a once-for-all transaction. Jesus makes that point plain: "If any one would come after me, he must deny himself and take up his cross daily and follow me" (Luke 9:23). Daily! Notice that. *Daily.* We may make a significant surrender today, but that surrender needs to be daily reconfirmed and daily implemented. Daily we need to say no to our own sinful selves and yes to the Father's will. But if we continually die to self, following the example of Jesus, then we may anticipate in faith a life of increasing spiritual productivity.

Are you and I willing to die to our self-centeredness, our self-concern, our self-conceit? Are we willing to die to our own plans and dreams and hopes if they are not for God's glory? Are we willing to pray sincerely our Lord's Gethsemane prayer? Are we ready to say yes to God's will and no to our own?

Death to the self-life is the price and precondition of spiritual productivity.

PRINCIPLE FOUR

A Disciplined Interaction with God's Word

FEW OF US ARE scholars. We are too busy being homemakers or breadwinners to invest long hours between book covers. But all of us recognize that books are life-enriching. They are sources of knowledge, entertainment, and inspiration. As Christians we are convinced that one particular Book has a value beyond all the millions of volumes in the Library of Congress.

We know that the Bible we love was written by men; in fact, we insist on that. But it is our conviction that the authors of the Old and New Testaments were so supernaturally guided that through their words and in their words we have the very Word of God. This is our conviction because it was our Lord's conviction, and after Him the conviction of the apostles. Paul spoke for himself and the entire early Church when he wrote to his son in the faith: "From infancy you have known the holy Scriptures, which are able to make you wise for salvation through faith in Christ Jesus. All scripture is God-breathed and is useful for teaching, rebuking, correcting, and training in righteousness" (2 Timothy 3:15–16).

Notice that according to Paul, Scripture is holy. It possesses a divine quality. Notice, too, that Scripture (Paul is referring to the Old Testament specifically, but what he affirms applies as well to the New Testament) makes us wise for salvation. Notice, further, that Scripture is God-breathed. The Holy Spirit so controlled the writers of the Bible that their words became God's Word. Finally, notice that because of its supernatural origin and authority, Scripture possesses a unique profit. We can sum up Paul's extraordinary claim like this. Here is a Book, really a library of sixty-six books, which, as we study it, can make us wise for *personal salvation, spiritual maturity*, and *fruitful service*.

Wisdom for salvation

Verse 15 affirms the first of these unspeakably valuable benefits. "Remember from whom your knowledge has come," Phillips translates the passage,

46

"and how from early childhood your mind has been familiar with the holy scriptures, *which can open the mind to the salvation which comes through believing in Christ Jesus.*"

This Book not only discloses God's ultimate purpose that will embrace the entire world, it also reveals to us a redeeming wisdom so vast and deep that it leaves philosophy and science in kindergarten.

Little wonder, then, that John Wesley, the founder of Methodism, a Spirit-filled revivalist who helped turn England from pagan darkness into a stronghold of Christianity, had this to say about the Bible:

> *To candid, reasonable men I am not afraid to lay open what have been the inmost thoughts of my heart. I have thought: I am a creature of a day, passing through life as an arrow through the air. I am a spirit come from God and returning to God, just hovering over the great gulf till a few moments hence I am no more seen. I drop into an unchangeable eternity. I want to know one thing: the way to heaven, how to land safe on that happy shore. God Himself has condescended to teach the way. For this very end He came down from heaven. He has written it in a book. Oh, give me that book. At any price, give me the Book of God. I have it! Here is knowledge enough for me.*

Wisdom for spiritual maturity

This Book can, as verse 17 teaches, make us wise for mature spirituality. God gave it to us as an instrument by which we, as men and women of faith, may become full grown, developing into Christlike disciples. We must not forget that maturity is a goal we never actually reach in this world. Maturity is not an end point; it is a process that goes on and on through all the years of our pilgrimage. Perhaps, then, we ought to think about *maturing* rather than maturity. Holding firmly to that distinction, let us observe how Scripture guides, instructs, and nurtures us in Christlike growth.

Notice the four phrases in verse 16. Paul writes that Scripture is profitable "for teaching, for reproof, for correction, and for training in righteousness." If we are to become more and more Christlike, there must be right belief that issues in righteous behavior. So when the apostle says that Scripture is profitable for doctrine, he is asserting that the Bible teaches us *what we ought to believe.* When he says that Scripture is profitable for reproof, he is asserting that through the Bible we learn *what we ought not believe.* When Paul says, furthermore, that Scripture is profitable for correction, he is asserting that the Bible teaches us *how we ought not behave.* When he says that Scripture instructs us in righteous living, he is asserting that the Bible tells us *how we ought to behave.* In short, Scripture teaches us *what to believe, what not to believe, how not to behave, how to behave.* We're further encouraged by this Book to expect that as we behave righteously because of our right belief, we will become more and more like Jesus Christ.

All of this sounds good and logical and neat. Some of us must admit, however, that it doesn't always work out quite so neatly as Paul seems to affirm. To be honest the Bible does not really speak to the issues we face. Scripture strikes us as rather irrelevant.

The reasons for this are by no means simple. One reason may be that our interaction with Scripture is *sporadic.* We read it in fits and spasms. We pick it up . . . once in a while. We turn to it . . . in times of crisis. As a rule, we "read over" Scripture; we glance at it casually, as most scan the stock market report in the morning paper. Maybe, then, Scripture does not contribute much of value to our experience because we interact with it sporadically and casually.

Besides that, some of us may approach Scripture pharisaically. We read it because we feel a sense of obligation. Or we read it to avoid a feeling of guilt. We are afraid that if we do not scan, say, three chapters daily, God is likely to chastise us. Or we read the Bible to acquire merit, accumulating a few more celestial brownie points. If that is how we interact with Scripture, we can hardly expect to find it a stimulating source of spiritual profit.

Here, then, are five simple suggestions that may transform our interaction with Scripture, changing a sporadic, casual approach into a profitable means of maturing grace. The first suggestion comes from Luke's action-filled first-century documentary—the book of Acts. Dr. Luke wrote about a remarkable group of believers in a town called Berea: "These Bereans were of more noble character the Thessalonians, for they received the message with great eagerness and examined

the Scriptures every day to see if what Paul said was true"
(17:11). Luke praises the Berean Christians because they
searched the Scriptures daily. This first suggestion may
be too obvious. But it's also too important to pass by:
Read God's Word regularly. Get into the pages of your Bible
every day. It doesn't matter whether you read ten
chapters or ten verses. What does matter is that you
practice steady, persistent interaction with God's Word.

The second suggestion comes from the psalmist:
"Oh, how I love your law! I meditate on it all day long"
(119:97). Thus, *read God's Word reflectively.* Tuck a text
away at the back of your mind. Then, when you have a
few moments by yourself and nobody else is clamoring
for your attention, bring that nugget from the
background to the forefront of your consciousness.
Meditate on it. Think about it—a phrase, a word, an
entire verse. But read God's Word reflectively as well as
daily.

The third suggestion comes to us in the form of a
prayer—also from Psalms: "Open my eyes that I may see
wonderful things in your law" (119:18). Therefore, *read
God's Word prayerfully.* This does not mean that we have to
offer a lengthy intercession whenever we pick up the
Bible. But it does mean that we ought to approach this
Book reverently, recognizing that it is something more
than a collection of human documents. This is God's
Word that has come to us through the agency of the
Holy Spirit, and we are not able to grasp its message
apart from the help of that same Spirit. Without the
insight He gives, we cannot see how the truth applies to

our own lives and how we can work it out in our behavior. That is why, when we read the Bible, there must be a prayerful recognition of our dependence upon the illumination of the Holy Spirit.

The next suggestion comes from the writer of Hebrews: "For we too have had a gospel preached to us, as those men had. Yet the message proclaimed to them did them no good, because they only heard and did not believe as well" (4:2 PHILLIPS). Whether we are listening to God's Word as it is proclaimed in church, or whether we are sitting at home reading the Bible by ourselves, Scripture will not profit unless our approach to it is one of believing confidence. Do we really believe that it is God's revelation? Do we really believe that God keeps the promises He makes? Do we really believe that God is serious about His warnings? Do we regard as truthful the things that we find recorded in this Book? Our fourth principle, then, is this: *Read God's Word believingly.*

The last of these five suggestions comes from the book of James. The apostle writes:

> *Don't only hear the message, but put it into practice; otherwise you are merely deluding yourselves. The man who simply hears and does nothing about it is like a man catching the reflection of his natural face in a mirror. He sees himself, it is true, but he goes off without the slightest recollection of what sort of person he saw in the mirror. But the man who looks into the perfect law, the law of liberty, and makes a habit of so doing, is not the man who hears and*

51

*forgets. He puts that law into practice and he wins
true happiness* (1:22–25 PHILLIPS).

Don't be forgetful! James urges us. Don't be like
someone who catches a glimpse of himself in a
department store mirror and then walks away with a
crooked tie and uncombed hair. In the same sense,
don't be a forgetful hearer (or reader) of God's Word.
Be a *doer* instead. Don't read Scripture to simply satisfy a
curiosity about the nature and purposes of God, *read it
to find out what He wants you to do.* And then, by His
grace, do it! *Read God's Word obediently.*

Here, then, are five simple suggestions. Interact with
the Bible *regularly . . . reflectively . . . prayerfully . . .
believingly . . . obediently.* Take these suggestions seriously
and you may find your vague disappointment with God's
Word melting away like frost in the morning sun. You
may discover—to your gratitude and delight—that this
magnificent Book really *does* speak to your daily
problems and needs. Far from being merely a source of
historical and theological information, it will become a
warm and welcome light for the dark road that winds
before you.

Wisdom for fruitful service

How does this affect our spiritual productivity? How
can it guide us into a life of active goodness that will be
for God's glory and the blessing of our neighbors?
Psalm 1 is the all-sufficient answer to this question.

Blessed is the man who does not walk in the counsel of the wicked
or stand in the way of sinners
or sit in the seat of mockers.
But his delight is in the law of the LORD,
and on his law he meditates day and night.
He is like a tree planted by streams of water,
which yields its fruit in season and whose leaf does
not wither.
Whatever he does prospers.
Not so the wicked!
They are like chaff that the wind blows away.
Therefore the wicked will not stand in the
judgment, nor sinners in the assembly of the righteous.
For the LORD watches over the way of the righteous,
but the way of the wicked will perish.

Here is the portrait of a person who delights in God's Word. He has learned to meditate reflectively on Scripture. And what is the outcome in his experience? He is like a tree firmly planted, not a reed shaken in the wind. His life is marked by stability. More than that, this person is productive. He bears fruit in his season. In addition, this person is marked by spiritual vitality. His leaf does not wither. Whatever he does prospers. Marked by spiritual stability, vitality, and productivity, he is authentically happy—truly and consistently joyful.

We must not take this psalm as a guarantee of a sizable bank account. The prosperity promised here is the same as that mentioned by the apostle John: "Dear friend, I pray that you may enjoy good health and that all may go well with you, even as your soul is getting along well" (3 John 2). John's concern is God's concern, a concern for our spiritual well-being. Certainly God cares about our needs for clothing and food. But He is even more deeply concerned about our relationship to Himself and our service for Jesus Christ.

If you and I share God's concern, we will not neglect a disciplined interaction with His Word.

PRINCIPLE FIVE

A Persistent Practice of Abiding

AN ATHEIST AND A CHRISTIAN were engaged in an intense public debate. On the blackboard behind the podium the atheist printed in large capital letters, "God is nowhere." When the Christian rose to offer his rebuttal, he rubbed out the "w" at the beginning of *where* and added that letter to the preceding word *no*. Then the statement read, "God is now here."

That is a true statement. God is. Now. Here. We say in our theological jargon that God is "omnipresent." There is no place where He is not. Everywhere and always in

55

time and space God is present. God was present before time and space existed. God will be present after history merges into eternity. We believe that. We also believe that God is present in Heaven as He is now present in time and space. He is present there with an intensity and fullness that it is impossible for us even to imagine. He is present there in a sort of dazzling, blinding, triple-rainbow of glory.

That is theology, of course, and fairly heavy theology. Yet what comforting theology! As we worship in church we remember and rejoice that God is now here. As we are at home with our families eating in peace and abundance we remember and rejoice that God is now here. Flying high above the earth, with the plane tossed about by turbulence and with lightning zig-zagging all around, we remember and rejoice that God is now here. Standing at the bedside of a friend who is desperately sick, or holding the hand of a precious child who may be near death, we remember and even then rejoice that God is now here.

So the doctrine of divine omnipresence, heavy theology though it is, proves to be a source of immense comfort in our troubled world.

As Christians we believe all of this. We also believe that since Jesus Christ is God, He is present everywhere. At the same time, however, we acknowledge that Christ, in the fullness of His grace and power, is present in the heart of the believer as He is not present in the life of the unbeliever. Illustrating this thought in a dramatic way, there is a portion of Scripture that ought to bring every sinner to his knees in surrender to our loving Savior. "Behold," the Savior says, "I stand at the door and knock; if any one hears My voice and opens the door, I will come in to him, and will dine with him, and he with Me" (Revelation 3:20 NASB). What a picture! Almost unbelievable. Jesus Christ is the all-powerful Creator, yet instead of smashing His way in He waits, humbly asking the sinful creature for entrance into his life. And what a picture of the intimate, incomparable fellowship that follows whenever anyone opens the door—Savior and sinner, Creator and creature eating together, enjoying heart to heart communion!

Paul, too, brings out this astounding truth in his letter to the Ephesian believers: "I pray that Christ will make His home in your hearts through faith" (Ephesians 3:17 GNB). And He does. Christ moves into our hearts as a permanent Resident when we invite Him to be our Savior and Lord. We may be unaware of His presence; we may not be conscious that He, living within us, has made our hearts His permanent home. Yet this is one of the mind-baffling marvels of the gospel: In His divine fullness and power and love our Lord takes up residence within the very life of every believer.

There is still another text that compels us to marvel: "Remain united to me, and I will remain united to you. A branch cannot bear fruit by itself; it can do so only if it remains in the vine. In the same way you cannot bear fruit unless you remain in me" (John 15:4 GNB).

What we have here is a two-sided truth: Jesus Christ lives in the heart of every believer, but it is the privilege of every believer to live in the heart of Jesus Christ. Whether or not we are conscious of this tremendous privilege purchased for us by the blood of the Cross, it is unshakably true. The Jerusalem Bible, a Roman Catholic version that is often remarkably insightful, translates this verse: "Make your home in me, as I make mine in you." These words help us grasp one side of this great two-sided truth of the gospel. Yes, Jesus Christ makes His home in the heart of every believer, but every believer can consciously and with grateful awareness make his home in the heart of Jesus Christ. And this challenging truth introduces us to a key principle for productive living: the steadfast practice of *abiding* in Jesus Christ. If you and I steadfastly abide, or remain, in Him, more and more of our Lord's character in all of its love and goodness will be developed and displayed in our own lives to the glory of God.

But this two-sided truth raises a two-sided question. What, for one thing, does it mean to abide in Jesus Christ? How, for a second thing, can you and I put this principle into practice?

Think about that first question. What does it mean to abide in Jesus Christ? Is it to remain loyal to His teachings? Is it, as we read in John 15:7, to grasp the words of Jesus, believing them and doing our best to obey them? Is it to have His teaching fleshed out in our lives? It is certainly all of these things, but it is that plus something else.

To abide in Jesus is to live in Him as a fish lives in the sea, a bird in the air, a branch in the vine. To abide in

Jesus is to be fully ourselves. It is to live out our own distinctive human lives while at the same time the fullness of Christ's life flows around us and into us and through us. How can we manage to comprehend this? I doubt that we can comprehend it, but we can surely understand the essential truth of this mystery.

All around us there are inaudible waves of sound and invisible waves of color, yet those waves remain inaudible and invisible unless we turn on the TV set and make the proper adjustment to a specific channel. Then sound, color, and meaning are suddenly there. What was invisible and inaudible becomes visible and audible; it becomes something that we can understand as well as see and hear. So the life of Jesus flows around us, into us, and through us. As we, therefore, make the proper spiritual adjustments, Jesus is more and more seen and heard in all that we are and say and do.

There is a second question, though, that may trouble us. How can we carry out this principle of abiding in Jesus to make our lives more productive? Can we do it by reading the Bible? Certainly that is an indispensable means, but something else is needed. Can we do it by praying? Yes, but something else is needed. Can we do it by worshiping and interacting with God's people? Yes, but once more there is a plus. You see, we cannot always be reading the Bible. We cannot always be praying. We cannot always be with fellow Christians. If you are an accountant, you must concentrate by the hour on ledgers with long columns of figures. If you are a teacher, you must interact with sensitivity to the pupils in your class. If you are a mother you must and you certainly ought to spend time homemaking, working out a budget, caring for your children, planning and preparing meals. Besides that, as Martin Luther argued, God does not want us to be spiritual recluses, withdrawn from the world. God wants us to be like Jesus. Read the Gospel, and where do you find Jesus? He is immersed in the stream of human life. He is mingling with the people, working, eating, laughing, holding babies. Imagine that! He is admiring flowers, watching birds, socializing with His friends, thankful to His heavenly Father for all the wonder of this world. He is reaching out in compassion to the sick and hungry.

How, then, do we carry out this principle for productive living? *We abide in Jesus Christ by developing a constant awareness of His presence.* The life of Nicholas Herman may help illustrate this thought. Born in France in 1611, he was admitted to the Carmelite community at the age of eighteen and was renamed Brother Lawrence. Before dying at the age of eighty, he wrote a series of letters that were collected under the title *The Practice of the Presence of God.* That small spiritual classic, first published in the seventeenth century, has been reprinted again and again.

What is the central and simple truth of that powerful little volume? Brother Lawrence learned that it is possible to develop a constant awareness of God. Constant awareness that God's life flows around us, into us, and through us. Oh, it took work. That is why he talks about the *practice* of the presence of God. Brother

Lawrence learned by diligence and discipline that we can be conscious of God virtually without interruption during all our waking hours. While he was cooking or when he was alone in his cell, that monk had as much consciousness of God as when he was worshiping in the sanctuary. He wrote:

> *The time of business does not with me differ from the time of prayer. And in the noise and clutter of my kitchen while several persons are at the same time calling for different things, I possess God in as great tranquility as if I were upon my knees at the blessed sacrament.*

That awareness required self-training. It required mental exercise. And, once again, practice, practice, practice. But Brother Lawrence learned the spiritual art of being aware of God's presence. And that is how you and I abide in Jesus Christ. We can develop a constant awareness of that mingling and merging of our lives with the very life of God.

Frank Laubach, the missionary we looked at in the third chapter, provides a more contemporary example. Called the "apostle to the illiterates" because he devised a system of teaching millions to read, he was an intimate friend of notables all around the world. He was also a prolific author and the recipient of dozens of honorary degrees. Laubach tells us how he learned to play *the game of the hours.* No matter where he was, no matter with whom he was, no matter what he was doing, he would

61

not let an hour pass without bringing the awareness of God from the background of his psyche to the forefront of his consciousness. As he matured in the Christian faith, he learned through unrelenting struggle to play *the game of the minutes.* He reached a state in his spiritual development that no matter what he was doing and no matter with whom he was talking, not a minute passed without his being aware of God's presence through Jesus Christ. He admits, as does Brother Lawrence, that this took intense self-training. It took discipline and diligence. It took practice. But Laubach insists that a steady God-consciousness can be cultivated by any believer.

My third example is a personal one, growing out of the relationship that has been central in my own life. My wife and I were married in 1939. Figure out, then, how long I have been blessed with a very loving, patient, self-effacing helpmate. I arise early and am off almost every morning for breakfast with a friend or a Christian group. Then usually I return home after six o'clock. We have supper, spending an hour or an hour and a half together. After that, I go to my study, leaving my deserted wife by herself. She assures me that I do not have to be in the same room with her, and I do not have to talk to her. The awareness of my presence transforms the home. She knows I am there, and that makes all the difference.

Do you and I live in the awareness that Jesus Christ, the omnipresent God, is around us and is within us? Are we aware that Jesus Christ in the marvel of His mercy has made our hearts His home? Do we rejoice in the inestimable privilege of consciously living in Jesus Christ while He lives in us?

Sit and reflect for a few minutes on this astonishing truth. You are busy, of course, and bombarded by stimuli. But try to sit in quiet reflection. Think about the wonder of God's grace. Jesus lives in me, and I can consciously learn to live in Jesus Christ! I can develop an awareness of His abiding presence. If I do—and as I do—I will have strength, peace, and comfort that would otherwise be impossible to experience. And I will become more spiritually productive to the glory of God.

PRINCIPLE SIX

A Vigorous Participation in Body-Life

GOD DOES NOT WANT Christians to be nomads, hermits, or recluses. He does not intend that we imitate the Lone Ranger, going it by ourselves without the help and ministry of our brothers and sisters in the faith. According to the apostle Paul, God's plan for human living is the opposite of an isolated self-sufficiency. The church, says Paul, is a spiritual body of interdependent members. "The eye cannot say to the hand, 'I don't need you.' And the head cannot say to the feet, 'I don't need you' " (1 Corinthians 12:21). On the contrary, Paul

65

insists, every member of the body needs every other member.

In the light of this great truth it might be good if we gave up singing one of the old spirituals:

> *On the Jericho Road,*
> *There's room for just two,*
> *No more and no less,*
> *Just Jesus and you.*

Think about it. If that song is right, we had better get off the Jericho Road. That is not the highway to glory because, as the New Testament repeats again and again, that highway is broad enough to allow all of God's people to march along together. Side by side. It might also be good to consign one of America's favorite hymns to the scrap heap.

> *I come to the garden alone,*
> *While the dew is still on the roses,*
> *And the voice I hear, falling on my ear,*
> *The Son of God discloses.*
> *And He walks with me, and He talks with me,*
> *And He tells me I am His own;*
> *And the joy we share as we tarry there,*
> *None other has ever known.*

Of course we can defend that hymn, appreciating its sincere sentiment. But it simply is not the norm for New Testament Christianity—Jesus monopolized by one believer in a lonely garden. The New Testament, John Wesley asserts, knows nothing of the solitary Christian. Wesley is right. New Testament Christianity is personal, but it is not individualistic. It is a fellowship of caring and sharing—a community of disciples who are interacting with one another in the body to which they belong. Christianity teaches that we need one another as much as the eye needs the hand and the head needs the feet.

All of us need our brothers and sisters in the faith if we are to develop into the productive disciples God wills that we become. That is one reason why across the centuries God's people have gathered together regularly for worship and fellowship. What was the practice of Old Testament believers? For an answer we consult the hymn book of the Jewish nation: "Blessed are those who dwell in your house; they are ever praising you! . . . Better is one day in your courts than a thousand elsewhere; I would rather be a doorkeeper in the house of my God than dwell in the tents of the wicked" (Psalm 84:4, 10). Even back in Old Testament times God's redeemed people joined together regularly with their brothers and sisters. This was their steady habit, a fixed part of their routine, as much as eating and sleeping. Participation in worship and fellowship was not like a second cup of coffee after dinner. It was the main course in life's banquet.

What was the practice of our Lord Jesus Christ when He was here on earth, walking the streets and hills of Palestine? "He went to Nazareth, where he had been brought up, and on the Sabbath day he went into the

67

synagogue, as was his custom" (Luke 4:16). Worship was our Savior's custom, His habit. He shared regularly in the fellowship of God's house with God's people.

What was the practice of the apostles in the earliest years of the church? It is Luke who tells us that "they devoted themselves to the apostles' teaching and to the fellowship, to the breaking of bread and to prayers . . . . Every day they continued to meet together in the temple courts. They broke bread in their homes and ate together with glad and sincere hearts" (Acts 2:42, 46). The early Christians practiced a daily fellowship that fostered gladness and sincerity, a fellowship that stimulated spiritual growth.

What then ought to be our regular practice? We have the Holy Spirit's unmistakable directive in the book of Hebrews: "Let us not give up meeting together, as some are in the habit of doing, but let us encourage one another—and all the more as you see the Day approaching" (10:25). We must not be careless about worshiping and fellowshiping with God's people. We must not be careless about participating in the body. It is God's appointed means of stimulating growth in grace. It is to be as much a part of our lives as eating and drinking—the main course. It is this participation and practice that motivates us to produce the whole cluster of Christlike characteristics that bring praise to God.

There is something highly significant about Paul's catalog of qualities in Galatians 5:22–23. The apostle speaks of love, joy, peace, patience, kindness, goodness, faithfulness, gentleness, and self-control. Do you see the key to these characteristics? These personality traits can be developed only through relationship and interaction with others. They cannot be developed by hermits. Lone Rangers needn't apply. Rugged individualists don't stand a chance. These exquisite character qualities develop nowhere except in the soil of community. If you wish, go off to some desert island and live by yourself. But if you do, you will never develop the fruit of the Spirit.

What is love? Very simply stated, love is caring for somebody else as much as I care for myself. How, then, can I expect to produce this characteristic if I isolate my life from other members of Christ's body?

What is joy? Joy is love rejoicing, but love cannot truly rejoice without other people. Selfishness can no doubt rejoice alone; love, however, cannot truly rejoice unless the rejoicing is shared.

And peace? Peace is love manifesting quiet tranquility, helping to create that same spirit among people.

Patience? Patience is love refusing to become frustrated.

Kindness? Kindness is love exercising compassion and forgiveness.

Goodness? Goodness is love aiming to be as gracious and generous as Jesus was.

Faithfulness? Faithfulness is love keeping its promises and sticking to its commitments.

Gentleness? Gentleness is love refusing to be harsh and demanding when it has every right to assert its own interests.

Self-control? Self-control is love voluntarily putting the brakes on its own feelings and actions.

All these Christlike characteristics are dependent upon the soil of interpersonal relationships. If we want to be fruitful we must make it our practice to join with our brothers and sisters in worship and fellowship.

How we need one another! Again and again the New Testament urges us to love one another. We are told that we ought to honor one another (Romans 12:10), teach and admonish one another (Colossians 3:16), serve one another (Galatians 5:13), bear one another's burdens (Galatians 6:2), tolerate one another (Ephesians 4:2), be kind to one another (Ephesians 4:32), and comfort one another (1 Thessalonians 4:18). By faithfully pursuing these responsibilities of mutual ministry we help one another grow in Christlikeness. More and more we become the productive disciples God wants us to be.

A Scottish pastor was concerned because a once-active member of his church was no longer participating in worship and fellowship. So on a winter night, he visited that spiritual delinquent in his cottage. With the fire burning on the hearth, the pastor and his parishioner sat there in typical Scottish fashion, saying little.

After a while the pastor remarked, "John, you have not been to church recently."

"I have been busy," John replied.

Nothing more was said as they continued to rock and stare into the fire. Finally, the pastor picked up the tongs and pushed one burning piece of wood off by itself.

Together he and John watched it. Slowly that flaming piece became gray and cold, no longer aflame. The pastor waited a few minutes, then pushed the piece back into the glowing heart of the fire.

Immediately it began to blaze once again. The pastor made no comment, but as he was leaving, his absentee member said, "Pastor, I will be back in the kirk Sunday morning."

We cannot be glowing, growing Christians if we neglect fellowship with other believers and fail to participate in the life of the body. How vigorously, then, are you and I putting this vital principle of productivity into practice?

PRINCIPLE SEVEN

A Diligent Cultivation of Roots

GOD WOULD NOT BE perfect if He lacked a sense of humor. So He probably smiled at the answer a little girl in Sunday school gave to her teacher's question, "Is there anything God cannot do?" All the children shook their heads no except that little girl, who vigorously shook her head yes.

"Susie," the teacher asked, "do you think there is something God cannot do?"

"Yes," Susie replied, "He can't please everybody."

Aside from that we must affirm that God can do

anything that in His wisdom and love He wills to do. Yet we realize there are many things God has willed to do only with our cooperation.

He has chosen to call us into partnership with Himself. He has chosen to entrust us with some limited responsibility. He has chosen to let us share in the fulfillment of His purposes and plans.

But if in laziness or unbelief or disobedience we refuse to cooperate with Him, God has willed to let us fail. He does not force us to be obedient. That explains why so many Christians never become spiritually productive. By grace through faith they have been born again, but after they enter into the family of God they stagnate. They do not cooperate with the Holy Spirit in His ministry of sanctification—the whole process of becoming more and more like Jesus.

There are believers who remain stunted saints until they die. They are saints; they have been born again, but they are immature and fruitless, unproductive plants in God's garden. They cannot blame Him for their failure. Heaven's scoreboard will show their own failures chalked up against themselves. They refused or neglected to cooperate with the Holy Spirit. They never developed roots.

Jesus refers sadly to such unproductive failures: "Those on the rock are the ones who receive the word with joy when they hear it, but they have no root. They believe for a while, but in the time of testing they fall away" (Luke 8:13).

How can we avoid the blight of fruitlessness? How

can we be productive? We must diligently cultivate roots. This is the principle that ties together all the other principles of spiritual productivity. It is impossible to produce Christlike characteristics without cultivating a deep, strong, God-relationship.

What hinders us, then, from cultivating a deep, strong system of supernatural support and supply? What holds us back from carrying out the other principles of productivity we have been examining? These are questions—troubling question—we need to ponder.

Now if we are righteous before God through faith, and if we are in a right relationship with God through obedience, that righteousness will reveal itself in spiritual productivity. Picture a sturdy apple tree weighed down in October with big, crisp, juicy Jonathans. What is the secret of its productivity? A strong root system. In your imagination walk all around that tree, scrutinizing it closely. Do you see its root system? No, that is an invisible source of support and supply. Yet without it the apple tree could never bear fruit. It would, in fact, wither away and die.

Transfer that principle to our own lives. Our God-relationship is invisible. You see me and I see you as human beings who confess Jesus Christ as Savior. But all we see of each other are the branches and the bark. I cannot see what goes on in secret between God and you. Neither can you see what happens in my God-relationship. You do not know and you cannot know the depth and strength of my devotional life—or perhaps its superficiality and weakness. In the same way I do not and cannot know about your devotional life. Each of us assumes that, because we are Christians, there must be an invisible system of supernatural support and supply that the other diligently cultivates. Yet in the end we can judge, as far as it is humanly possible and permissible, the vitality of a believer's God-relationship by the quality and quantity of fruit produced in his life. As Solomon puts it, "The root of the righteous yields fruit" (Proverbs 12:12 NASB). We see fruit and conclude that the fruit-bearer has a right relationship with God, a relationship supported and nourished by spiritual roots.

Why are we rootless?

As we ponder the problem of spiritual barrenness among self-confessed Christians, three reasons for the failure to cultivate a strong root system seem to surface: ignorance, indifference, and ingratitude.

Ignorance

Perhaps we honestly do not understand that our cooperation is indispensable in this business of developing roots. We may wrongly imagine that God does everything by Himself to make us more Christlike. And since He does everything, we need do nothing. So we sit and wait for spiritual fruit to mature spontaneously in our lives. We expect it to take place effortlessly and automatically.

In the past Soviet teachers tried hard to destroy any faith in God in the impressionable minds and hearts of school children. The atheistic teachers first selected two plots of ground. After carefully plowing the first plot, they made sure it was fertilized, planted, watered, and weeded. They called it the "Government's Garden." The other plot was not prepared. Instead, the teachers scattered an abundance of seed on the hard surface of the soil. It was called "God's Garden." What happened? The Government's Garden produced an abundance of fruits and vegetables. God's Garden produced nothing except a tangle of weeds. With this graphic bit of "evidence" before their eyes, the Soviet children did not have to be lectured concerning the truth of atheism. God's unproductive garden proved His nonexistence. What those Soviet educators did not realize or admit, however, is that in gardening God chooses to work through human cooperation. And so it is with spiritual productivity. If we fail to cooperate or refuse to cooperate, our gardens will grow weeds instead of produce. We will not bear fruit for Him.

If we have been ignorant of our responsibility, then it is time we reviewed a very pointed message from the book of Hebrews:

> *You seem so slow to grasp spiritual truth. At a time when you should be teaching others, you need teachers yourselves to repeat to you the ABC of God's revelation to men. You have become people who need a milk diet and cannot face solid food! For anyone who continues to live on "milk" is unable to digest what is right—he simply has not grown up. "Solid food" is*

only for the adult, that is, for the man who has developed by experience his power to discriminate between what is good and what is evil (5:11–14 PHILLIPS).

Spiritual maturity, steady growth in Christlikeness with ever-increasing productivity, comes from training, practicing, doing. It comes from cultivating the roots of our God-relationship and cultivating those roots diligently.

We must not subscribe, then, to the old Soviet view of how God acts in the world. Instead, we must subscribe to the view of the reverent doctor who says, "I dress the wound; God heals it." God may very well choose to heal miraculously. But under normal circumstances God does not heal unless we use whatever medical resources are at our disposal. And that is the key: God acts in response to our own action. So if we have not understood this fact before, we can no longer enter the plea of ignorance about our own personal responsibility in spiritual fruitbearing.

Indifference

Despite the full awareness that our cooperation is required for growth in Christlike maturity, we may not want to give it the time, energy, and attention that are essential. The bottom line becomes a question of values. What is of supreme importance? What really matters? What is at the top of life's agenda? Do we give more time, attention, and energy to socializing, vocational advancement, TV, stamp collecting? How high on our scale of values do we place our relationship with God? If we put it on a low level, then of course we do not feel compelled to work at it diligently. We can push it aside with a yawn. Put yourself right now in Southern California. Are you there? Good. Now find yourself in an orange orchard. The trees are literally weighed down with fruit—an astonishing bumper crop. Can you visualize it? The owner of that orchard, however, is in desperate financial straits. He simply must have the money those oranges will bring. But as night descends, the air grows chilled. The weatherman forecasts frost and as you stand in the orchard you can feel it coming. You overhear a voice—the voice of the owner speaking to his wife.

"Oh well," he says. "We won't worry if the oranges freeze. We won't worry if we lose our home. We won't worry if we lose everything we have worked for all these years. Sure, we could stay up all night. We could light the smudge pots. We could fight the frost. But why bother? It really isn't worth the effort. Let the oranges freeze."

"Oh, no!" his wife exclaims. "We can't afford to lose this crop. We have to save it!"

This good wife knows the value of that potential harvest and fortunately her common sense prevails. The couple does everything possible to protect that precious fruit. They work together feverishly, this man and his wife, from dusk to dawn. Forgetting their weariness, they pour all their energies into a battle to save those oranges.

You don't blame them, do you? Neither does God.

79

Fade back from California to wherever you are reading and thinking. Forget that imaginary orchard and concentrate on the garden of your life. How much do you value your relationship with God? Is it worth more than all the orange groves in California? Is it worth the investment of five minutes a day? Is it worth ten minutes? Is it worth half an hour? Is it worth the investment of your attention and energy? Or do you rank your relationship with God far down on the scale of values and thus treat it with indifference?

Are you spiritually fruitless? Or are you less fruitful than you could be because you are spiritually lazy? Indifference, plain laziness, may be the cause of your failure—or mine—to be more productive.

Ingratitude

An unthankful spirit, an unappreciative heart, may be still another cause of our fruitlessness. We may be like the Israelites. Ingratitude was their besetting sin. We read in the Old Testament how God had done for His people everything He could do. Can you hear the pathos in God's voice when He asks the Israelites: "What more could have been done for my vineyard than I have done for it? When I looked for good grapes, why did it yield only bad? Now I will tell you what I am going to do to my vineyard. I will take away its hedge, and it will be destroyed; I will break down its wall, and it will be trampled" (Isaiah 5:4–5). Plainly those Israelites were ungrateful. They did not thankfully acknowledge the goodness and the mercy of God who had led them out of Egyptian captivity.

Let us refrain from throwing stones at those ingrates back in Israel. What about you and me? Think of all God has done for us in Christ. Think of how He has redeemed us at the measureless cost of Calvary. Think of God's mercy, goodness, and love. Think of God's grace. Think of what we owe to Him. We are hopelessly in debt to God for His salvation! Motivated, then, by an overwhelming sense of gratitude, we ought to do our best to please Him, and nothing pleases Him more than our spiritual productivity.

A deep and secret spring

St. George's-by-the-Vineyard, according to Richard Wentz, is an old church in the foothills of the Allegheny mountains. It holds the title deeds to a vineyard that produces, the natives insist, the most luscious grapes anywhere in that region. Every year when those grapes are ripe, members of St. George's come to pick and eat the luscious clusters or to make wine that is allegedly the best available anywhere. People often wondered about that vineyard because nobody in particular seemed to take care of it. Then old Jeremy, the sexton, died. His father before him had been sexton, and his father's father before him. No one could remember a time when the sexton of the church had not been a member of that family.

A taciturn recluse, Jeremy did not talk much to anyone, but he very lovingly cared for St. George's-by-the-Vineyard. After his death, a note was found alongside his bed. It simply said, "The key to everything is under the altar." So the senior warden went to the altar and looked underneath. There surely enough was a key, but not only a key; there was a stone slab that could be lifted, and below the slab there were stairs leading down into a crypt. The warden and some of the other officials took flashlights and began to investigate that dark cellar. To their surprise they could hear the gurgling of a spring. And when they reached it, they discovered beside it a chart and a time schedule. Unknown to anyone else, the sexton had been releasing the waters of that spring regularly and faithfully into the ducts that irrigated the vineyard. That was the secret of its rich productivity—a spring that people did not know about, a secret source of renewal and vitality.

How spiritually productive are our vineyards? How fruitful are they? Is there a hidden Spring from which water flows abundantly into our lives, producing a rich harvest of Christlike characteristics?

PRINCIPLE EIGHT

A Willing Cooperation with the Pruning Process

SOME OF MY FRIENDS have been blessed with that proverbial green thumb. Their vegetable gardens look like pictures out of a seed catalog. Their fruit trees are things of symmetry and beauty and they yield fruit by the bushel. I hesitate, therefore, to discuss "pruning," because I have never done it. But there is no getting around it. Pruning is one of God's essential methods for stimulating spiritual productivity. Cooperation with His pruning process is indispensable if we are to bring forth

Christlike fruit. Jesus Himself highlights this principle: "My Father is the gardener. He cuts off every branch in me that bears no fruit, while every branch that does bear fruit he prunes so that it will be even more fruitful" (John 15:1–2).

One day I was visiting Wasco, California, in the bountiful Kern Valley. My host, a master grape-grower, escorted me through acre upon acre of lush vineyards. He pointed out some of the choice varieties, boasting that they had been imported originally from Italy and France. Then he explained pruning, which, he insisted, is absolutely necessary. You must get rid of dead branches, cutting the vines back ruthlessly, or they will not be productive. Most people, he remarked, are afraid to prune ruthlessly (a process that demands real skill). Nevertheless, this radical approach to pruning is the secret of a rich, abundant grape harvest. Sometimes, however, even with ruthless pruning a vine fails to respond. In that case there is nothing to do except cut it off and burn it up.

I have never forgotten my friend's short lecture on gardening. In fact, every time I read these words of Jesus that conversation comes to mind. As the divine Gardener cuts away at the dead wood of our lives, we must willingly cooperate with that pruning process.

How does God prune us?

You and I are not unconscious branches. We are conscious human beings, formed in the image of our

Creator. We are called upon to respond to Him in faithful and submissive obedience. When God graciously prunes us, He does not use a knife. Instead, He works through the circumstances of our lives. Whenever He detects in any one of His children the potential of productivity, He starts to shape that Christian's experience in such a way as to cut out the dead wood that is hindering growth and fruitfulness. A disciple with spiritual potential may suffer a crushing disappointment. He may undergo a jolting loss. He may find himself on a hospital bed with a painful illness. He may taste the bitterness of betrayal by a trusted friend. He may stumble like a zombie through the breakup of his marriage. He may weep over a wayward son or rebellious daughter. He may walk through the darkness of the valley of death, bereaved and heartbroken. He may know the misery of loneliness. He may even feel the agony of despair. In those circumstances he may keep on asking why. "Oh, God, why? Why is this happening to me? Are you angry? Are you displeased? Are you punishing me?"

And God may answer lovingly: "No, my child. This is pruning, not punishment."

Let us reflect for a moment. Have you or I been living in a blast-furnace of affliction? Have we been passing through a dark river of suffering? Have we struggled to stay afloat in a turbulent flood of trouble? Have we been under pressure that we can scarcely tolerate? And have we been tempted to interpret all these testing circumstances as punishment? Then we need to change our viewpoint and shift our perspective.

We need to look at these testing circumstances from another angle of vision. Perhaps God has not been punishing us. He has been pruning us. He has used the sharp knife of painful circumstances to do it. *Not punishment, but pruning!*

Think of a student staring at a picture in a psychology text. He scrutinizes it one way and insists it is the profile of a rather haggard old lady; but suddenly, while he continues to gaze at that picture, there is a split-second alteration, and now he beholds a lovely young woman. It is the same picture seen differently. And that is what we need, a changed perspective. We need to see all of our faith-testing experiences from the standpoint of our Lord's Words: "Every branch that does bear fruit he prunes so that it will be even more fruitful" (John 15:2). Not punishment, *pruning.* The Master Gardener uses the pruning shears of painful experience to stimulate our growth and productivity. He uses it because no other method really works. And we must not forget that He uses it precisely when He detects in some believer the potential of fruitfulness.

But caution is in order. We had better not pray for increased spiritual productivity without considering the effect of the pruning process. That is the strong advice of Dr. Andre Bustanoby. He was enjoying a productive ministry in Richmond, Virginia, when his attention was gripped by John 15:2. So repeatedly he prayed that God would prune his life to make him even more fruitful. As if in answer to that prayer, he was invited to a much larger church in California that held out the prospect of enlarged usefulness. But after he moved there, circumstances did not go well. Andre's relationship with his wife, Fay, started to deteriorate as he and she quarreled often and angrily. And the deterioration of his marital relationship affected the whole range of his pastoral relationships.

One morning there was an ugly scene between that Christian couple. Andre stormed out of the house, drove to his church, and sat in his study so disturbed and disgusted that he put his head on his desk and began to weep. Then he took out pad and pen and began to write a long letter to Fay, venting his bitterness and resentment. Fay, however, had followed him to the church and entered his study just as he finished writing. He thrust the letter into her hands.

Fay read it and shook her head sadly. "Honey," she said, "you need help."

"I need help!" he sputtered. "I need help? Not me!"

He was an outstanding preacher, a bestselling author, a victorious Christian. He in need of help? Unthinkable! Yet he did need help and eventually secured it from a counselor who himself had been a pastor. He found it, too, in a therapy group. At first, his attitude in that group had been one of pride, disdain, superiority, and self-sufficient aloofness. One day, though, the group went to work on him, lovingly, but with relentless candor. Andre broke. Emotionally shattered, he somehow managed to get home where he wept and wept in his wife's arms, begging her forgiveness. God had answered Andre's prayer for pruning. Today he and his wife are happy and fulfilled in a joint-counseling ministry, coauthoring helpful books and testifying that God, through painful circumstances, can make us productive. Dr. Bustanoby still prays for pruning. But having felt the sharpness of the growth-producing knife, he now asks, "Please cut me gently, Lord."

Why does God prune us?

A passage in the book of Hebrews helps us understand why our loving Lord uses the razor edge of painful circumstances so ruthlessly on the living tissue of our daily lives. Please read these words carefully, as though you were seeing them for the first time.

> *My son, do not make light of the Lord's discipline, and do not lose heart when he rebukes you, because the Lord disciplines those he loves, and he punishes everyone he accepts as a son.*
> *Endure hardship as discipline; God is treating you as sons. For what son is not disciplined by his father? If you are not disciplined (and everyone undergoes discipline), then you are illegitimate children and not true sons. Moreover, we have all had human fathers who disciplined us and we respected them for it. How much more should we submit to the Father of our spirits and live! Our fathers disciplined us for a little while as they thought best; but God disciplines us for our good, that we may share in his holiness. No discipline seems pleasant at*

the time, but painful. Later on, however, it produces
a harvest of righteousness and peace for those who
have been trained by it (12:5–11).

Notice the apostle's emphasis on discipline, a grossly misunderstood element in wholesome child-training. Wise discipline is positive, not negative. It is any means or method employed to modify a child's behavior constructively and mold his character morally. The purpose of the parent's discipline, therefore, is upbuilding rather than punitive. What, then, is God's purpose? Let's look again at verse 10:

For our fathers used to correct us according to their own ideas during the brief days of childhood. But God corrects us for our own benefit, so that we may share his holiness (PHILLIPS).

Divine discipline is not punishment. It is pruning designed to produce holiness. And to be holy is to be Christlike, to be conformed to the Jesus model of loving and being. Holiness is a personality structure and a behavior pattern that give flesh to the fruit of the Spirit. So the purpose of pruning is not to cut us down, as if God took delight in breaking our hearts, frustrating our hopes, and dashing our dreams on the rocks and failure. His purpose in pruning us is to stimulate the development of holiness that yields a rich harvest of Christlike characteristics.

Years ago I forged a friendship with a seminary student who was one of the finest Christians I have ever met, a student who has become an extraordinarily

89

Christlike man and whose ministry has been immensely blessed. But in the course of his theological training that student hit an emotional snag and went into a psychological tailspin. Hardly able to function, he was heading toward a breakdown. Mine was the serious responsibility of counseling with him. Day after day we talked and prayed together, working through his problems. Vividly I remember some of those sessions when, weeping, in pain, he would exclaim, "Why is God letting me go through this? Why?" I could only assure him of my deep conviction that God had a wise and loving purpose in view. And He did. That student emerged from his emotional crucible like refined gold, with a depth of understanding, compassion, empathy, trust, and commitment that was simply phenomenal. His life has had a spiritual impact upon thousands of people, at home and overseas. That is the purpose of God's pruning: to stimulate the growth of Christlike holiness, leading to spiritual productivity.

Can God's pruning fail?

God . . . fail? Heresy! How could one use those two words in the same breath? He is the almighty Creator, the sovereign Lord of everything, the Ruler of ocean and earth and skies. Anything He does must be a glorious success. Whatever He wills cannot be frustrated. Agreed. But what has God willed?

He has willed, first of all, to save us *without our cooperation*. "For it is by grace you have been saved, through faith—and this is not from yourselves, it is the gift of God—not by works, so that no one can boast" (Ephesians 2:8–9).

On the other hand God wills to sanctify us only *with our cooperation.* What, then, if we respond to His pruning with rebellion or stubborn disobedience or maybe even unbelieving bitterness? What if, as God applies the knife of painful circumstance, we grumble, kick, doubt, and resist? What then? We will shrivel spiritually and forfeit the possibility and privilege of productivity.

There is a thought-provoking, disturbing example of how this can happen in the book of Isaiah.

> *I will sing for the one I love a song about his vineyard: My loved one had a vineyard on a fertile hillside. He dug it up and cleared it of stones and planted it with the choicest vines. He built a watchtower in it and cut out a winepress as well. Then he looked for a crop of good grapes, but it yielded only bad fruit. "Now you dwellers in Jerusalem and men of Judah, judge between me and my vineyard. What more could have been done for my vineyard than I have done for it? When I looked for good grapes, why did it yield only bad? Now I tell you what I am going to do to my vineyard: I will take away its hedge, and it will be destroyed; I will break down its wall, and it will be trampled. I will make it a wasteland, neither pruned nor cultivated, and briers and thorns will grow there. I will command the clouds not to rain on it"* (5:1–6).

91

This parable shows what happens when God's people respond in sinful disobedience. But why did the Israelites respond in this way? Remember Dr. Bustanoby's experience. Pruning is painful. It means humiliation, the surrender of our human self-sufficiency, the loss of what we prize. Forget the Israelites. What about ourselves? When the Master Gardener applies the knife of ego-deflating circumstances, are we willing to hold still? Are we willing to submit? Are we willing to pray, "Cut me, Lord. Please cut gently, but prune away the deadness."

Are we willing to exercise patience? Are we willing to walk on faithfully in the darkness? Are we willing to forgive the very people who hurt us the most? Are we willing to let God train us how to endure, how to be thankful in adversity, how to rejoice in tribulation, how to forget our own needs and in love reach out to the needs of our neighbors near and far?

If we are willing to cooperate with our Father, the Master Gardener, the pruning process will not be a failure.

It is the branch that bears the fruit
That feels the knife,
To prune it for a larger growth,
A fuller life.
Though every budding twig be lopped,
And every grace
Of swaying tendril, springing leaf,
Be lost a space.

92

O thou whose life of joy seems reft,
Of beauty shorn,
Whose aspirations lie in dust,
All bruised and torn,
Rejoice, tho' each desire, each dream,
Each hope of thine
Shall fall and fade; it is the hand
Of Love Divine
That holds the knife, that cuts and breaks
With tenderest touch,
That thou, whose life has borne some fruit,
May'st now bear much.

—Annie Johnson Flint

PRINCIPLE NINE

A Ruthless Elimination of Thorns

THORNS, writes Charles Swindoll, are

> *Little things.*
> *Things that prick, penetrate*
> *. . . and progressively poison.*
> *Unexpected things.*
> *Low-lying vines that trip, tangle*
> *. . . and eventually imprison.*

Thorns are those growth-stifling habits that block and limit our progress toward a Christlike maturity. The failure to identify and eliminate such choking vines can devastate our spiritual productivity. As a result, some Christians move all through the years of their pilgrimage, producing at best scrawny, sickly fruit. And at worst, nothing but leaves.

What are those thorns?

What, then, are these patterns of attitude and behavior that sap the vitality from our growth in Christ? Our Lord's parable about a sower who scattered seed on four different sorts of soil may provide some helpful clues.

> *A sower went out to sow his seed, and while he was sowing, some of the seed fell by the roadside and was trodden down and the birds gobbled it up. Some fell on the rock, and when it sprouted it withered for lack of moisture. Some fell among thornbushes which grew up with the seeds and choked the life out of them. And some seed fell on good soil and grew and produced a crop—a hundred times what had been sown . . . .*
>
> *This is what the parable means. The seed is the message of God. The seed sown by the roadside represents those who hear the message, and then the devil comes and takes it away from their hearts so that they cannot believe it and be saved. That sown on the rock represents those who accept the message with great delight when they hear it, but have no real*

root. They believe for a little while but when the time
of temptation comes, they lose faith. And the seed
sown among the thorns represents the people who hear
the message and go on their way, and with the worries
and riches and pleasures of living, the life is choked
out of them, and in the end they produce nothing.
But the seed sown on good soil means the men who
hear the message and grasp it with a good and honest
heart, and go on steadily producing a good crop
(Luke 8:5–8, 11–15 PHILLIPS).

The thorn of cares and worries

In verse 14 Jesus puts His finger, first, on cares—the worries of this life. He warns against the danger of letting legitimate responsibilities degenerate into growth-smothering obsessions. Now of course it is right for us to take our responsibilities seriously. Indeed, we must. It is right for us to devote ourselves to essential concerns, the obligations that we believe God has assigned to us. It is right for a father to take conscientiously his responsibility to provide everything that his family really needs. That is a legitimate concern. It is perfectly right, also, for a mother to take conscientiously her responsibility of homemaking and child rearing. That is surely a legitimate concern. It is right for a college student to take conscientiously his responsibility to read required texts and write reports—an entirely legitimate concern. *But when conscientious care degenerates into excessive and obsessive carefulness, it can become a growth-choking thorn.*

97

That was the trouble with Martha, the sister of Lazarus and Mary—a very conscientious woman to whom we are introduced in Luke's gospel.

> *As they continued their journey, Jesus came to a village and a woman called Martha welcomed him to her house. She had a sister by the name of Mary who settled down at the Lord's feet and was listening to what he said. But Martha was very worried about her elaborate preparations and she burst in, saying,*
>
> *"Lord, don't you mind that my sister has left me to do everything by myself? Tell her to come and help me!"*
>
> *But the Lord answered her, "Martha, my dear, you are worried and bothered about providing so many things. Only one thing is really needed. Mary has chosen the best part and it must not be taken away from her!"* (10:38–42 PHILLIPS).

Reading this account, most of us probably sympathize with hardworking Martha and have some negative feelings toward lazy Mary. But as we reflect on the actions and reactions of these two sisters, we must conclude that Martha had her priorities badly twisted. She was so obsessed with preparing a good meal that she bypassed the opportunity to enjoy a spiritual feast. Can you see her bustling around the kitchen, worried that the roasting lamb would not be tender or the bread would not be baked on time? All the while, care-filled and fretful, she was missing out on fellowship with Jesus. A well-meaning human being with lopsided values, poor Martha was obsessed with care about things that are far lower than secondary. Can it be that she cared too little about the things that matter most.

Could it be that you and I have become like Martha . . . with a warped sense of values . . . twisted priorities . . . a heart that is anxious and filled with care about secondary things? Are we, in fact, so obsessed that we have little or no time for fellowship with Jesus? Has that kind of growth-choking thorn been turning the garden of our lives into a jungle of weeds?

The thorn of riches

Jesus next warns against the danger of letting an excessive concern for money making become a growth-choking obsession. To consider this hazard I turn to Paul's first letter to Timothy, extracting from it a pair of contrasting texts. First, the apostle solemnly declares that "if anyone does not provide for his relatives, and especially for his immediate family, he has denied the faith and is worse than an unbeliever" (5:8). It is our God-assigned responsibility to provide adequately for that circle of human beings who depend on us for life's necessities. That is an unavoidable responsibility. If we willfully shirk this, we are sinning. Now, compare that warning with this further instruction:

> *People who want to get rich fall into temptation*
> *and a trap, into many foolish and harmful desires*
> *that plunge men into ruin and destruction. For the*

> *love of money is a root of all kinds of evil. Some*
> *people, eager for money, have wandered from the faith*
> *and pierced themselves with many griefs* (6:9–10).

Suppose we love money—really love it. Suppose we covet the luxuries money can buy or the influence that money provides. Suppose we trust in money. Suppose we view money as the ultimate source of security and happiness. Suppose that money, instead of serving as a means for doing God's will and blessing God's people, becomes our god. Suppose we share the perspective of the rich fool of Luke 12 and become so obsessed by the love of money that we have no concern for God or for neighbors near and far. If that is how we are, money has become a thorn to us. Unless uprooted, it may be turning the garden of life into an ugly mass of unproductive weeds.

> *And he said to his disciples, "Therefore I tell you,*
> *do not worry about your life, what you will eat; or*
> *about your body, what you will wear. Life is more*
> *than food, and the body more than clothes . . . . Your*
> *Father knows that you need them. But seek his*
> *kingdom, and these things will be given to you as*
> *well"* (Luke 12:22–23, 30–31).

The thorn of pleasure

Jesus also puts His finger on pleasure, warning against the danger of letting its pursuit become a strangling, life-sapping thorn. He warns against possible

100

obsession with hobbies and sports—any and all relaxing and recreative activities that can degenerate into pastimes that take priority over everything else.

We need to understand clearly that God is *not* an enemy of pleasure. He is *not* a killjoy. We need to italicize that fact especially for the sake of teenagers. God is *not* down on music, skiing, humor, hunting, art, fishing, drama, and jogging. God is *not* down on TV as such any more than He is down on checkers. God is not down on moral sex. Once in a while, reading Christian books and listening to negative sermons, we might pick up the opposite impression. God seems to be down on anything pleasurable. What a sad caricature of our loving Creator! Take a careful look at Paul's guilt-relieving assertion: "Command those who are rich in this present world not to be arrogant nor to put their hope in wealth, which is so uncertain, but to put their hope in God, who richly provides us with everything for our enjoyment" (1 Timothy 6:17). Rejoice that the Holy Spirit put such a liberating text in the Bible! God richly provides us with everything for our enjoyment." He does not want us bored by monotony. On the contrary, He wants us to have experiences of sheer ecstasy—and satisfying moments of quiet delight.

What happens, though, when golf, let's say, pushes God aside? What if we spend far more time perfecting certain strokes than we spend in prayer? What happens when any activity, whether it is writing poetry or riding horseback, becomes an all-consuming passion that takes precedence over everything else? At that point, a

101

legitimate pleasure—something good in itself—has become an obstructive thorn that makes the garden of life spiritually unproductive.

Riches and pleasures are good. They are God's gracious gifts intended to make human experience happy and fulfilling. By sinful mutation, however, they can mushroom into growth-choking excesses.

Has that sinful mutation taken place in our discipleship? Have we been tolerating the insidious development of destructive thorns in the inner gardens of our lives? Have we allowed our values to be distorted, our priorities twisted? Have we let riches and pleasures degenerate into obstacles that hinder our growth and progress in Christ? Is that the reason why we have been spiritually unproductive, or perhaps less productive than we ought to be? A yes answer means that today—today, not tomorrow—you and I must swing into action.

Today, not tomorrow, is the time to pour out our hearts in honest confession: "Lord, I have been failing . . . miserably. My life has not been much of a garden at all—let alone a fruitful, productive one. To be honest, Lord, it's been more like a weed patch. Forgive me, Father, and help me begin now—today—dealing with my behavior and changing it."

What behavior? It may be the habit of laziness. It may be an attitude of self-indulgence. It may be preoccupation with responsibilities in home or business or school. Whatever it may be, take it before Him. "Lord, help me. Help me to rethink my values. Help me to reorder my priorities. Help me to reschedule my time. Help me use

102

the spade of stubborn discipline. Help me use the hoe of strenuous and sustained effort. Help me use the weed-killer of intercession. Motivate me to go to work on those growth-choking thorns in the garden of my life." If from the heart we pray like that, we can be fully assured of God's help.

Before he became a world-famous novelist, A. J. Cronin was a physician in his native Scotland, attached to a hospital staff. A girl from the Highlands was there in training—awkward, clumsy, and slow. Late one day, after a tracheotomy had been performed on a patient, that student nurse was assigned to monitor him through the hours of the night. It was her responsibility, if the tube in the man's throat began clogging up, to clean it out and prevent him from choking. As the hours wore on, the tube did clog up. The patient began choking—desperately gasping for air.

Suddenly overcome by a wild panic, the girl forgot her instructions and raced through the hospital looking for Dr. Cronin. Eventually she found him, and, breathless, managed to sob out the situation. Cronin raced to the patient's room—but arrived too late. Seething with anger, he dragged the girl down into his office and proceeded to tongue-lash that weeping student nurse. "You are through," he told her. "I'll see to it that you are dismissed." The girl, however, sank down on her knees, "Please, Doctor, for God's sake give me another chance," she begged. "Give me another chance!" The obvious sincerity of the woman, her heartbroken repentance, touched Cronin's heart. He

103

pleaded her case, and she was allowed to stay on. Given another chance, she became an outstanding nurse; in fact, a superintendent of nurses.

There are those times, fellow-pilgrims, when I look back critically at my own career. How grateful I am for any fruit that I may have been able to bear! Yet I see my relative lack of productivity, and convicted of sinful failure I pray, "God, give me another chance. Lord, if there are weeds or thorns that are preventing the growth of spiritual fruit, help me deal with them. Help me go to work and get rid of them."

God wants to give all of us another chance. Do not think He has run out of patience. He has not. But perhaps this very moment we ought to pray, "Gracious Lord, give Your servant another chance . . . another chance to face those deep-rooted weeds and deal with them in the power of Your mighty Spirit. Allow me the privilege—even at this crossroads of my life—to bear fruit for you."

PRINCIPLE TEN

A Truceless Warfare with the Little Foxes

SOME CHRISTIANS THINK that Song of Solomon ought to be eliminated from Scripture. It is much too frank. It is too sensual and erotic to suit their sanctified tastes. But there it is, one of the sixty-six books in the library of revealed truth; and its timeless message helps us catch a glimpse of human love from God's perspective.

One particularly compelling verse from that book will help us focus on a final principle:

Catch for us the foxes, the little foxes that ruin the vineyards, our vineyards that are in bloom (2:15).

We do not have to know much about foxes or vineyards to understand this verse. Foxes are mostly meat-eaters, but they also eat plants. In the early spring they bite off the new tender shoots, gnaw away at the roots of the vines. That is why they are destructive pests. And that is why those who are concerned about the productivity of the vineyard must engage in a truceless warfare against them.

When you think about it, those little foxes do not seem particularly dangerous. They are small—by no means as strong as a coyote or a bear. You can't really compare them to some rampaging bull elephant in Africa that tramples down a missionary garden. Yet those little foxes are capable of doing terrible damage. Quit driving them out, and see what happens? They burrow and gnaw until vines wither and die.

This simple text gets right to the heart of the whole matter of spiritual productivity. What blights our lives? What hinders us from bringing forth the Christlike fruit of love, joy, peace, patience, kindness, goodness, faithfulness, gentleness, and self-control? What blights our marriages and distorts that most significant union? What blights our families and hinders our homes from being places where that Christlike fruit is flourishing? What blights our churches and keeps them from becoming more dynamic centers of witness and service? It is not likely to be some gross evil or some dark

106

depravity. The strong probability is that a few little foxes are running loose and doing their destructive damage. Perhaps instead of recognizing how lethal these small, rather weak animals can be, we ignore them—watching instead for a coyote or bear to show up. Meanwhile the gnawing and the burrowing go on, and only too late we may wake up to the deadly peril of the little foxes.

A fox called "self-centeredness"

Self-centeredness is only a little fox, but it can cause terrible damage to a life, to a marriage, to a family, or even to a church.

But what's so bad about it? What could be so damaging about the Me-First attitude? It is not a vile sin—Me First. It is not some gross evil—Me First. It is not some sort of dark depravity like child abuse or adultery. The Me-First attitude is just a common, harmless weakness. Call it pride. Call it ambition. Call it egotism. It is only a little fox, not a rampaging bull elephant. Yet what terrible damage can be done by self-centeredness. The self-centered person thinks only about his needs, his wishes, his feelings. The self-centered person ignores other people and their needs, their wishes, their rights, their feelings.

This individual may not be blatantly ruthless. He may be very polite. But underneath that facade there is no sincere concern about anyone else. He or she is like a character in a once-popular novel about whom the author writes, "Edith was a little world, bounded on the north, south, east, and west by Edith." Change the name to Jim or Janice. It makes no difference. The all-controlling attitude, the bottom line concern is . . . Me First. Not only me first, but Me Last. Me always. I count. Nobody else does. That spirit gnaws away—like a little fox—at the roots of our relationships. It can make a marriage miserable. It can create civil war in a family. It can breed disharmony in a church. And oh, how that little fox gnaws away at the roots of our God-relationship! It needs to be dealt with *ruthlessly*.

A fox called "bitterness"

This little fox, too, is able to do appalling damage. Once again, it may not impress us as a serious fault. It is not a horrendous sin or gross evil. What is so bad, so desperately bad about bitterness, a negative, critical, angry spirit? Or what is really so harmful about being jealous and resentful? What is wrong? Well, one might as well ask what is dangerous about a little cyanide. It doesn't take much to choke out a life.

Years ago a friend of mine called my attention to a text in Hebrews. We had eaten lunch together and then walked out into the parking lot of the restaurant, continuing to talk. Opening his King James Bible, that man of God called my attention to chapter 12, verse 15, which he read with unforgettable earnestness: "Looking diligently lest any man fail of the grace of God; *lest any root of bitterness springing up trouble you, and thereby many be defiled.*" Time after time I had read that text, but never before had I been struck by its true significance. Bitterness! Smoldering resentment! An angry, negative, hostile spirit! That does damage, terrible damage. Like acid, destructive negativism eats away at the heart of a man or woman. Bitterness poisons life both personally and interpersonally. Among its victims are marriages, families, friendships, and churches.

A Midwest merchant had twin boys. They were identical and inseparable from birth. They dressed alike and they did everything together. In fact, they never married. After college they came back home and took over their dad's business. They worked so harmoniously that everyone in the community pointed to their relationship as a model of creative cooperation.

One morning, however, a customer came into their store and made a small purchase. The brother who served him took the dollar bill, put it on top of the cash register, walked with the customer to the front of their establishment, and after he left, went back to deposit the money. But the dollar bill was gone. So he asked his brother, "Did you put a dollar bill in the cash register?"

His twin answered, "I didn't see any dollar bill."

The first brother was surprised. "That's funny. I distinctly remember that I put it on the cash register."

A little later he asked again, "Didn't you take that dollar bill and put it in the cash register?"

His twin replied somewhat testily, "No. I told you before that I didn't see it."

Tension developed between those brothers over that dollar bill. Every time they discussed the matter, there were charges and countercharges. The brew of bitterness became more and more vile. Eventually they broke up their partnership and split the store right down the middle, each brother owning his half. The community was drawn into the quarrel. For twenty years those two men and dozens of other people were troubled by dark resentment and deep, smoldering rage.

Then one day a stranger drove into town. He came to the store that had been divided down the middle, walked into one side, and asked the white-headed proprietor, "How long have you been in business here?" The twin told him. "Well," the stranger replied, "then I've got something I must square with you." Twenty years ago, he explained, unemployed and homeless, he had been wandering around the country. One morning he had dropped off a freight train in that little town and walked down a back alley hoping to find something to eat. Through the open door of a store he had seen a cash register with a dollar bill on top. Nobody was there; only two men up in the front. He sneaked in and stole the dollar bill. But brought up as a Christian, he had been bothered by guilt, so he finally decided to return, confess his theft, and pay whatever the store owners thought was due to them.

As he talked, the white-haired man listened with tears running down his cheeks. When he was able to recover his composure he said, "Please come with me. I want you to tell the same story to my brother." They walked into the other half of that divided store, and before long the white-haired twins were weeping in each other's arms. Twenty years of hostility! Twenty years of resentment! Twenty years of cold silence and lingering loneliness!

Bitterness. Just a little fox. But who can calculate its devastation?

Have we been permitting that little fox to invade the vineyards of our lives? Have we been excusing our bitterness by thinking that a little resentment, a little anger, a little hostility is really harmless? Have we been rationalizing, arguing that the little fox of bitterness is not as destructive as a coyote or a bear . . . or a rampaging bull elephant? Let us not be fooled any longer. Marriages can be wrecked by bitterness. Families can be made wretchedly unhappy by bitterness. Churches can be undermined by bitterness. Let us deal ruthlessly with this little fox.

A fox called "unforgiveness"

There is a third little fox that comes out of the same litter as the foxes of self-centeredness and bitterness. Where you find one, you'll always find the others. You'll find malice and gossip. You'll find a desire to hate, hurt, belittle, and humiliate. And finding these, you'll be as far as you can get from the Spirit of Jesus Christ. For on the cross, in all His agony, our Savior prayed, "Father, forgive them."

Let me tell you about another pair of brothers in the flesh—who professed to be brothers in the faith. These brothers were residents of a tiny Western town. Both of them were deacons in the town's only church. One day they had a fierce quarrel. Neither would ask the other's pardon. Neither would deal with the little fox of unforgiveness. So they lived on as neighbors, never speaking to each other. When Sunday came, one would sit on the north side of the little church, the other on the south side. Once a month, as is the practice in their denomination, the Lord's Supper was observed. As deacons, those brothers served the bread and the cup, symbols of our Lord's reconciling death. But as soon as the benediction had been pronounced, one brother went out the side door while the other one left through the front door. Unforgiving and unforgiven, they made that sacrament of reconciliation a blasphemous mockery. Is it any surprise that the brothers were terribly unhappy, their families miserable, and their church permanently blighted? Is it any surprise that an effective witness for Jesus Christ was nullified in that little town?

But what about ourselves? Perhaps that malicious little fox is being allowed to eat away at the roots of our human relationships, even our relationship with God. Did I say "little" fox? Its appetite is as vast as hell itself. Drive it out! Catch it and kill it! Do not wait until tomorrow.

A fox called "thoughtlessness"

There is still one other little fox that may be burrowing and gnawing away at the roots of our lives. It is the little fox of thoughtlessness. Thoughtlessness, well, that is something trivial, isn't it? At worst, just a trifling fault. Can't we ignore and forget it? By no means! Remember, this fox comes from the same litter as self-centeredness, bitterness, and unforgiveness. When we are self-centered, self-absorbed, and self-preoccupied, we are unconcerned about anyone else's needs, wishes, and feelings. It is thoughtless selfishness and selfish thoughtlessness that make us inconsiderate, insensitive, unkind, and uncaring. It is what hurts our mates. It is what embitters our families. It is what alienates our friends. That little fox of thoughtlessness can do life-destroying damage. Then, after the harm is done, we wake up and start to offer our lame excuses . . . too late.

I didn't mean to leave you out. I didn't mean to make that cutting remark. I didn't mean to forget your birthday. I didn't mean to do those things. I was so busy it never crossed my mind. I intended to visit my friend before he died. I intended to write a letter. I intended to telephone. I intended to witness. I intended to pray. I was so busy that I never got around to carrying out my good intentions.

This little fox can be extremely destructive, because thoughtlessness betrays an unloving and sinful self-centeredness.

Dr. C. Roy Angell was holding an evangelistic crusade in a large church. On Sunday morning he told how the famous author, Thomas Carlyle, married his own secretary. But Carlyle was thoughtless, absorbed in his own interests and activities, treating his wife as if she were still his employee. Stricken with cancer, she was confined to bed for a long time before she died. After her funeral, Carlyle went back to his empty house. Disconsolate and grieving, he wandered around downstairs thinking about the woman he had loved.

113

After a while he went upstairs to her room and sat down in the chair beside the bed on which she had been lying for months. He realized with painful regret that he had not sat there very often during her long illness. He noticed her diary. While she was alive, he never would have read it, but now that she was gone he felt free to pick it up and thumb through its pages. One entry caught his eye: "Yesterday he spent an hour with me, and it was like being in heaven. I love him so much." He turned a few more pages and read, "I listened all day to hear his steps in the hall, but now it's late, and I guess he won't come to see me." Carlyle read a few more entries, then threw the book on the floor and rushed out through the rain back to the cemetery. He fell on his wife's grave in the mud, sobbing, "*If only I had known. If only I had known.*"

After telling that story Dr. Angell dismissed the congregation. As people were leaving the church, he walked down the center aisle and noticed in the last pew a woman with two little boys. She was crying. He sat down beside her, and between sobs the woman was able to share her grief. She was married to a pharmacist, a man she was sure loved her and their sons deeply. But he was so busy, up in the morning before the children, working until 9:00 at night, working on Sundays, too. Because the boys almost never saw their father, the mother would sometimes take them down to the store in the afternoon, and they would just walk around through the aisles hoping to see their dad.

"Dr. Angell," she said, "he's promised that he'll come

114

to church tonight. Will you tell that story about Carlyle again?"

Dr. Angell thought to himself, "People will laugh at me for being absent-minded if I do that." But he agreed. He would tell the story again, explaining to the congregation that he was doing it by request.

"Oh, no!" the woman protested. "My husband is a very smart man. He'd know that I'd put you up to it. Will you just tell the story as if you'd forgotten to do it this morning?"

Reluctantly, at the risk of gaining an undeserved reputation for premature senility, Dr. Angell agreed.

That night in the service there were the man, his wife, and their two boys. Dr. Angell again told about Thomas Carlyle and his heartbroken regret, "If *only I had known! If only I had known!*" When the service was dismissed, the family of four still sat in the pew, and the father was weeping. As Dr. Angell talked with him, the man exclaimed, "I thank God I've come to know before it's too late. Things are going to be different." Dr. Angell reports that things have indeed been different. Every Christmas that pharmacist sends him a huge box of candy with the note, "Things are still different."

"If only I had known" can usually be translated into "If only I had *thought.*" It is thoughtlessness, self-centered thoughtlessness, that causes hurt and sadness. It is a little fox that does unimaginable damage to life's vineyard.

Let us volunteer as recruits in a truceless war against the little foxes of self-centeredness, bitterness, unforgiveness, and thoughtlessness. Perhaps the first piece of action in this war will be to apologize to a wife, telephone an offended church member, or visit a neglected friend.

Whatever it takes, God help us to drive out the little foxes. If we do, life can become a fertile garden for the glory of our Lord.

The Oswald Chambers Library

Spiritual guidance from the author of *My Utmost for His Highest.* Powerful insights on topics of interest to every believer:

If You Will Ask

Reflections on the power of prayer.

The Love of God

An intimate look at the Father-heart of God.

The Place of Help

Thoughts on daily needs of the Christian life.

Not Knowing Where

Keen spiritual direction through knowing and trusting God.

Baffled to Fight Better

Job and the problem of suffering.

Bringing Sons into Glory/Making All Things New

A challenging compendium on the life of Christ.

The Shade of His Hand

A penetrating look at the book of Ecclesiastes.

Order from your favorite bookstore or from:

DISCOVERY HOUSE PUBLISHERS
Box 3566
Grand Rapids, MI 49501
Call toll-free: 1-800-283-8333

Note to the Reader

We set our minds in doing the Will of God, obeying him even tho obedience involves _self-denial_; (the surrender of anything that would interfere with the fullfillment of God's divine purpose.)

Death to the self life is a condition of spiritual productivity.